Disrupt From Within:

How to engage your internal team's creative power
to protect market share, strengthen defense,
and avoid stagnation!

Justin Waltz

Disrupt From Within:
How to Engage Your Internal Team's Creative Power to Protect
Market Share, Strengthen Defense, and Avoid Stagnation.

Copyright © 2018 JUSTIN WALTZ INC

JW@JustinWaltz.com
www.JustinWaltz.com
www.disruptfromwithinbook.com

ISBN-13: 978-1978057531
ISBN-10: 1978057539

Printed in the United States of America.

DISRUPT FROM WITHIN

How to engage your internal team's creative power
to protect market share, strengthen defense,
and avoid stagnation!

JUSTIN WALTZ

*"If you don't disrupt yourself, someone will
disrupt you, for you."*
—Mark Randolph, Co-Founder, Netflix

*"The responsibility of leadership is to not
come up with all the ideas.
The responsibility of leadership is to
create an environment in which
great ideas can thrive."*
—Simon Sinek, Author, Start With Why

*"The people who are crazy enough
to think they can change the world
are the ones who do."*
—Steve Jobs, Founder, Apple

Contents

Preface ix

Foreword xi

Part 1: The Innovation Storm 1

A note from the author: 3

Introduction 7

Chapter 1: Pre-Storm: Agenda, Problem Statements,
Growth Strategies 17

Chapter 2: Pre-Storm: Defining The Scope Of Work 31

Chapter 3: The Innovation Storm 35

Chapter 4: Post-Storm 41

Bonus: Implementation -Ideas must be adhesive 51

Bonus: Destroy your one-page plan annually 55

Appendix: Innovation Storm Problem Statements 57

Appendix: Innovation Storm Optional Supplies 59

Appendix: One-Day Innovation Storm Facilitators Guide 63

The Facilitator Guide for the Day of the Storm 65

Appendix: Final Tips for Facilitators 73

Appendix: Innovation Storm Internal Announcement
Memo Sample #1 (intro from outside facilitator) 75

Innovation Storm Internal Announcement Memo Sample #2 .. 79

Bonus: Exponentially Grow Your Work & Your Business
with a Virtual Team 81

Part 2: Peer Performance Groups 91

A note from the author 93

Chapter 1: Who needs a group? 101

Chapter 2: Peer Performance Groups: A history lesson 105

Chapter 3: An ounce of prevention is worth more than
a pound of cure 109

Chapter 4: The structure – The business/non-profit peer
performance group 113

Chapter 5: The agenda for the peer performance
group meeting 119

Chapter 6: Keeping it fresh and adding even more value,
year after year. 147

Appendix: Who can benefit from a peer performance group 175

Appendix: Benjamin Franklin's Junto – questions to start
discussion: 181

Appendix: Questions to dive deeper in your off time 185

Appendix: Top 10 ice breakers to open a meeting with
vulnerability 187

Appendix: The four mindsets of every successful peer
performance group 189

Appendix: Finding retreat homes, cabins, lodges,
experiences, and activities 193

Appendix: A conversation about space, creativity, and time ... 195

Appendix: It is essential to teach peer performance group
members to set S.M.A.R.T. goals, and how to make them
S.M.A.R.T. 197

Appendix: The host's presentation guidelines & question/
answer suggestions to provoke thought 199

Appendix: Peer performance group example recruitment
letter/benefits of a peer performance group 213

Sources and Inspirations 215

Acknowledgements 219

About the Author 221

Innovation Storm Guest Facilitation 223

Preface

THANK YOU FOR picking up my book! I am honored that you have opened this page. Welcome to my world. This book is divided into two parts with bonus sections to help you disrupt your organization, implement change, and then build systems to hold yourself accountable as well as create accountability groups so everyone is holding everyone accountable, inside and outside of your organization. Accountability is a beautiful thing.

The first part of this book is going to talk about one of the biggest opportunities and one of the most impactful days any organization can have. A day the entire organization can get together and create an environment to discover disruptive and impactful ideas to 10x the organization and embrace the future. It is an extremely effective team building event, and I recommend you hold at least one per year. We call this an "innovation storm," and I hope you enjoy the first part of this book that describes in detail how to execute an effective innovation storm. If you are not an expert facilitator, or do not have one in your organization, in the back of the book you'll find an opportunity on how to reach out to me and my team for professional facilitation. We look forward to hearing from you.

In Part Two of this book, I am going to share with you the

secrets to successfully building peer performance groups in any organization, trade group, or industry.

Peer performance groups date back to the first real records of history, and almost every successful business, entrepreneur, athlete, musician, or professional can relate to a peer performance group. The ultra-successful do not do it alone, and neither should you. In Part Two, I am going to show you exactly how to build peer performance groups, how they should be executed, and what to expect in these groups.

My writing style and tone are designed to direct you, the reader, to take action or assign someone to execute the ideas written in this book with haste. I provide details, agendas, and formats that allow you to take these systems and put them to work. Do not forget environment and leadership are critical to each of these systems. The ability to inspire and create an environment where ideas and individuals can flourish will be critical to the success of each of these tools.

I love that you have picked up my book… I envy all of you who are taking action and putting these systems into place. Please email me at JW@JustinWaltz.com to send photos, videos, and stories about the meetups you are holding so I can post them to our social platforms, and I can share in the joy you are going to have and the success you will have within your organizations after implementing these systems.

I am extremely envious I cannot be at each one of the events you are going to be holding after reading this book, so please include me in them by sending me snippets of your events!

Good luck and go crush it!

Justin Waltz

Foreword

ONE WEEKDAY AFTERNOON a few years ago, I was 3,000 miles from home spending some quality time with a small group of our Valpak Seattle associates, winding down after a day-long program I had led.

Soon after we arrived in the hotel bar, a stranger (not from our group) seeing our identical logoed polo shirts walked up to me and asked, "Are you the boss?"

"Kind of," I said. "How can I help you?"

"I just want to shake your hand, my friend. I found a $100 check in my Valpak envelope a couple months ago. I took it to the bank and it was real! I couldn't believe it—it was real money in the mail!" he said.

It may not sound like it, but randomly inserting "real" $100 checks in Valpak envelopes mailed across the country was a big idea that made our product better and also made a lot of consumers opening their blue envelopes very happy for years.

This simple idea came from a brainstorming session.

"Simple and brilliant," I said when the idea hit our whiteboard.

"Radical and dangerous," responded the Accounting Department.

It turned out to be simple and brilliant after all.

I can almost guarantee that the best new ideas to take your company or organization forward already exist inside your company.

Somebody has already had those ideas but has never spoken up.

That person might be your most experienced and longest employed executive… but just as likely could be somebody who joined your organization yesterday morning.

Sally in your Accounting Department may secretly think she has some cool marketing ideas for your company (and she actually has them), but thinks nobody would take her marketing ideas seriously.

Sam, a worker on your factory floor, may have an idea for a new product, better packaging, or a great way to cut costs, but nobody will listen because he is "just an hourly worker."

I have seen these ideas emerge dozens of times, and they often come from the lips of the least expected people.

But it goes much deeper than that.

More than twenty-five years ago Robert J. Kriegel and Louis Palter wrote a real classic, *If it Ain't Broke...Break It!: And Other Unconventional Wisdom for a Changing Business World.*

It is old, yes, but I still recommend it. Especially when times are good and your organization is on a roll—your job as a leader is to create opportunities for your team to reach for disruptive ideas that may be so radical that they would disrupt your comfortable, contemporary, and profitable world.

So why do it?

Isn't it better for you and your people to come up with those disruptive ideas *before* your competition does? Or worse yet, before somebody else way off your radar screen wipes you off the face of the Earth, maybe not only taking you out, but all of your competitors as well?

It happens, you know.

Discovering these truly big ideas that "Disrupt From Within" requires much more than dumb luck.

More than an Employee Suggestion Box in the lunch room.

In *Disrupt From Within*, Justin Waltz gives you a practical tool kit you can easily implement to create a powerful idea-generating engine within your organization that may truly change your world and everyone else's too.

Joe Bourdow

Joe Bourdow is Managing Partner of Premier Franchise Advisors LLC, a firm owned by several top leaders in Franchising. The firm provides board memberships and help with franchise leadership, private equity, and capital investments. Bourdow and his partners formed PFA, following Joe's retirement from Valpak. Joe is the former President of Valpak and Executive Vice President of Cox Target Media, the parent company.

Joe spent the first 18 years of his career as a radio station owner and manager and multi-unit franchisee of Valpak and Fastsigns.

PART 1
The Innovation Storm

A note from the author:

L
OOK... IF YOU aren't taking action, making bold moves, and asking hard questions, you will get swallowed up. In a year or a decade or a few decades, but it will happen. This book is a no-nonsense, cut to the chase, how-to guide to having one of the most powerful days your organization has had since its inception. This book is for those who are ready to disrupt themselves before someone else will... The ideas to save your business and propel your future are in the minds of your front-line team members, within your middle management, and your executive team. Bring in your board of advisors, if you want, your mother-in-law—who knows? The ideas are out there. Implementation comes next... but first, let's get the ideas out of the brains of your organization.

I want to thank all of those around me who believe in me, tell me to keep going, inspire me to fight through the daily emotional ups and downs of leadership and entrepreneurship, and all my fellow colleagues that inspire me to keep working hard. You all really motivate me to bring the energy day in and day out.

I also want to point out three resources and books that inspired this guide to take place. First off, I attended a training series by the YPO (Young Professional's Organization) on best practices for inspiring innovation in organizations. After this, I realized there was a huge opportunity to break down how to facilitate an innovation storm into a simple, easy to follow formula with guides and agendas. David Silverstein hosted the webinars and inspired me to write this guide so people could get started quickly on a one-day storm and disrupt their own businesses right away. David Silverstein, Phillip Samuel, and Neil DeCarlo are the authors of *The Innovator's Toolkit*, which is packed with 50+ techniques to grow your business and innovate your products or services. I highly recommend this book to keep the momentum going in your organization.

If you truly enjoy the idea of disruption and changing your business, while learning more about the art of innovation, I will recommend two books. These books have changed the way I see business, the way I see music and fine art, and they motivated me to keep going by following my passions and spinning out ideas. First, I recommend you read *Exponential Organizations* by Michael Malone, Salim Ismail, and Yuri Van Geest. I cannot say enough about this book; it will change the way you see the future of global businesses. Next, I recommend reading *Originals: How Non-Conformists Move the World* by Adam Grant. This book travels down the path of success stories and debunks the myth of overnight successes. It shows the amount of work our idols have put in, and encourages you to stay out there and keep working. This book was a huge inspiration for me wanting to show others how to execute an innovation storm, as well as it helped me understand the creative process of the people we consider legends in business, music, and art. I recommend you pick up this book if you are as inspired by me about the strategy and theories around generating disruptive ideas.

Now it's time to get to work. If you are skeptical about the entire day, or about blocking off your entire company for one day, I have three words for you: **Trust the process**. If you execute the agenda outlined in this book, follow the detailed instructions, and create a crazy fun environment, you will walk away with a stronger team and killer ideas. I promise you will change your organization forever! I will see you on the other side of million-dollar ideas! Enjoy the ride!

Lastly, I am envious and jealous I cannot be a part of every single innovation storm, because the amount of fun and the ideas that are produced are extraordinary, and to be a part of the chemistry that is created during the innovation storm is truly an amazing experience. I hope you enjoy this game changing day and implement this as part of your annual planning strategy each year.

– Justin Waltz

Introduction

THE BOOK TITLE "Disrupt From Within" is meant to encourage leaders to look within first, because the teams within the team have ideas that need to be heard. Our teams within our organizations speak with our clients and customers, and are closest to the front lines. The greatest asset in your organization are the ideas that are in the minds of your team members to improve, change, eliminate, or disrupt your organization and industry. In this book, I describe an innovation storm as one of the biggest days of the year your organization will have. It will become an annual tradition. It will be so much fun—it will launch your teams to take major action, and it will be so impactful it will land on the calendar annually, if not two to four times per year. I encourage you to make this a big event, supported by all, because ideas that are not just shared by all but created and lived by all, are ideas that will be executed at the highest levels. We will dive into the innovation storm in Chapter 1.

The book's subtitle says exactly what is going to happen during this planning day. You will engage your entire team's creative power. Not just upper level management, not just middle management and front lines, but the entire team. This is a chance for upper management to hear from the front lines, middle management to voice their ideas to upper management, and, most importantly, the front-line team members to share their thoughts and ideas. Some real gems will come from this planning day.

Besides engaging your team, you will strengthen your market share, protect yourself from competition and industry disrupters, and avoid plateau or stagnation. Complacency is not something you want in today's world, and, as mentioned in the book *Exponential Organizations*, every CEO should replace their title with CXO, Chief Exponential Officer. Every leader should be looking to exponentially disrupt their organization, because if you aren't, someone else will do it for you. Not just your business, but your industry. So, go be the leader that you are, and disrupt your organization and hopefully your entire industry, and let's change the world and have some fun!

WHAT THE HECK IS AN INNOVATION STORM?

An "innovation storm"—also known as a "design storm," "nerd jam," or an "idea jam"—is a collaborative brainstorming event intended towards generating quantum ideas in a fun and creative setting. Innovation storms take place in large groups with a facilitator and an agenda. The format of a storm is flexible to the goals identified and the disruptive space that is being attacked.

I was recently listening to a conference of pool store owners (companies that service and build residential swimming pools). The owners were performing an innovation session together, a quick innovation storm. This group of swimming pool store owners came up with an opportunity for a smartphone app which would involve taking your smartphone outside to capture a picture of your backyard. Once the app receives the picture of your backyard, it will immediately process a display of your backyard and any type of pool would be transposed onto the image. Next, you would have the opportunity to select from various types of pools to be installed. The app would show a picture of your backyard and each type of pool installed into your backyard with some basic information and stats about the pool you've selected. If you like the pool design, the application will give a ballpark estimate to have the pool installed. If you like what you see, you simply click "submit," and your information will get submitted to pool companies that choose to be a part of the app network.

The above represents an innovative idea, and it has been quite disruptive to the residential pool marketing and technology space. Maybe the "Uberization" of the pool industry?!

You hold innovation storms around technology, around your existing service business or internal operations. You could explore how to support your employees or franchisees, or go completely disruptive and come up with new ways to approach your client base or new markets to enter.

The innovation storm is fundamentally a one-day summit with a few critical events before and after the actual day. This guide is going to describe exactly how that day will go and how to facilitate that day. You have three choices when executing the innovation storm. You may choose to facilitate your own innovation storm, volunteer someone from your team to learn the art of executing the innovation storm, or seek outside facilitation. We will always recommend an outside facilitator (and more reasons why will come later), but no matter the choice you make, there will be plenty of tools available for you to download to help you. We will provide tips, an agenda, appendices, and handouts to help you execute your own innovation storm at the end of this guide.

A note on the facilitators you choose to run your meeting...

Regardless of how you choose to execute your innovation storm, all facilitators should have empathy for their meeting attendees. A strong facilitator will execute a meeting with these things in mind: all meetings need to be fun, action packed, energetic, and have a specific agenda. We are going to show you how to execute this meeting and how to facilitate a successful innovation storm.

In this book, I will teach you specifically about the one-day innovation storm... let's get started!

Don't forget to download all the samples and worksheets at www.disruptfromwithinbook.com.

LET'S EXPLORE DEEPER INTO WHAT AN INNOVATION STORM IS.

An innovation storm is a high-energy, entertaining, and collaborative session which involves getting everyone together in your organization. It is a fun-filled team-building event with the expectation of coming up with 10x and 100x ideas to grow your business and bring out the next million-dollar improvement or disruptive technology. The goal for the storm is to come up with a vast amount of opportunities for your organization to disrupt your market and gain new business. These opportunities are either to grow and add to your existing business, to grow your existing customer base, or to completely disrupt your market. Additionally, there may be opportunities to enter into a new market or do something completely unconventional from your current organizational model. Think about the Uberization of the taxi cab industry. Think about putting a man on the moon, self-driving and electric cars. From modern streaming subscription-based music to the personal computer, these disruptive innovations have changed our lives.

The above disruptive innovations came from internal minds, from organizations all over who brought these ideas to market. Even the Starbucks Frappuccino was originally discovered by a group of baristas testing new products in their own store in Southern California. A regional manager then brought the idea to the Starbucks executive team. Now the Frappuccino makes up close to half of Starbucks coffee revenues during summer months. What is your Frappuccino? Who will bring your next Frappuccino to the table? An innovation storm will provide this opportunity.

The innovation storm is an opportunity for everyone in the organization to come together. An innovation storm is a culture-building event where employees get to step outside their day-to-day activities, spend time in thought, and be heard in an inspiring space. It could be three or more people in the organization that get together for one day. I suggest up to 50 people may participate. *Any more than 50 people will make for a longer day, so you may want to hold two or more storms depending on the size of your group.*

Depending on the structure of how you choose to set up the day, your innovation storm may last four to five hours. This is an opportunity to utilize a key team-building exercise by creating an environment of "nameless and rank-less feedback." You are creating an opportunity where anyone in the organization can share an idea, no matter their title, tenure, or rank. *It is critical that you point this out while setting the stage for a successful day. This will ensure ideas are flowing and everyone participates.*

WHY YOU SHOULD PLAN YOUR ONE-DAY INNOVATION STORM

The innovation storm is a great team collaboration tool where *everyone* in the organization gets together and works to share best practices and ideas... every single person in the organization, from the owner to the internal administrators, to customer service and customer-facing roles.

The rules are simple. There are no negative actions allowed and immediately any negativity gets killed. As part of an appendix, we have included the Innovation Storm Tool Kit that contains a bullshit flag, a bell for ringing if someone breaks a rule, silly string, and pipe cleaners for creating an inventive atmosphere. And since this book was written in 2017, and fidget spinners are huge right now, they can be included in the kit. They make great toys for the day, as well as a slinky or two.

The innovation storm provides an opportunity for you to look at your business from a high level and include a wide variety of internal experts. For those who do not spend their days making changes or adapting the business model, this is a big opportunity to learn about the business and suggest change. Topics discussed during the innovation storm include: why we do what we do, what exactly do we do, and what issues and barriers might the consumers run into. These are all critical components in creating an environment where the best ideas rise to the surface, all of which we will explore as we get further into this book.

The goal of the innovation storm is to come up with ideas that are going to change the business one year, three years, and ultimately ten years from now. It is an immense opportunity to bring the organization together. It is an entertaining, animated event that specifically should have a spirited facilitator.

A STRONG FACILITATOR

A strong facilitator is a must to execute a strong innovation storm. An outside facilitator (external to your organization) has proven even better than an internal facilitator—this is a person who will not be afraid to ask questions and will not know the difference between a basic question and one that participants know the answer to. Seeing a problem from the outside is one key to creating a disruptive environment. Additionally, the owner of the company or leader of the innovation storm should never double as the facilitator; they must be part of the innovation storm as a participant.

The key to exploring the furthest depths of innovation involves an outside facilitator for a few reasons. A talented facilitator is able to push the team to go further and ask questions that will challenge the current business model and explore opportunities untouched. An excellent facilitator will explore the above, all the while keeping the meeting flowing, gratifying, and engaging.

A gifted facilitator will involve music, breaks that are appropriately timed, snacks, beverages, and coffee. You may decide to have fidget spinners, silly string, or pipe cleaners. *See the appendix at the end of the book for the Innovation Storm Tool Kit.* By creating a fun learning environment, coupled with a talented facilitator, you will foster an atmosphere for original feedback and participant engagement.

As the promoter of the innovation storm (and the reader of this book), you should immediately get started generating buzz around the innovation storm that is about to take place in your organization. Let's begin rallying the team; everyone in the organization should be participating in your innovation storm.

In this book, we will teach you how to be a world-class innovation storm facilitator. Thus far, we have covered what the innovation storm is and why now is the best time to hold your innovation storm. Now let's get into what exactly the day looks like.

The space and the day – What does it look like? What do I need?

The innovation storm will be a group of people in a larger creative space or office suite. We recommend your meeting be offsite where team members can get together but be away from the day-to-day distractions of business operations. It is essential that the space be an inspiring space. A fun conference room, a larger office, or think creatively… maybe a museum, chamber of commerce building, or we have even seen events take place in a brewery! There are so many cool spaces out there. You may want to consider renting a big house on Airbnb or VRBO.com, which can be very affordable. Also consider a Google search of "co-working" in your local city, and you will find affordable office spaces and conference rooms for rent. These are typically very inspiring, creative spaces and one of our favorite solutions. *We owe a debt of gratitude to Station House St. Pete, in St. Petersburg, Florida, for their creative environment, where much of this book was written and edited* (http://stationhousestpete. com/). Bottom line: you are not required you use a hotel conference space or an office space. **Be creative.**

For your innovation storm, you will need whiteboards, markers, note paper, and sticky notes. We recently had an innovation storm where we had a whiteboard measuring 25 feet long and 8 feet tall. We filled the entire board, ran out of space, and had to keep erasing content and questions. *Take photos of any notes before you erase them.* You want to have a large whiteboard and plenty of scrap paper because your team will want to scribble notes and ideas that are flowing at a rapid pace. Sticky notes, markers, silly string, pipe cleaners, spinners, bells, BS flags, pens, and note pads should all be on the desks or tables spread out so that everyone has materials to utilize. Encourage a fun and energetic environment with music playing, and they should be throwing things at each other—we even encourage having paper airplanes for the paper pilots in the room.

You need to create a fun and enthusiastic team environment where people can be original. Inspire participants to dress for enthusiasm and creativity. Some people might want to dress formally while others may choose to dress comfortably. It depends on what they feel. As the main promoter and/or facilitator of this creative day, you should be ready to support an environment where people feel relaxed, confident, and inventive.

PROMOTING YOUR INNOVATION STORM

You should make it a goal to promote the idea storm weeks in advance. You want to inform all team members what is coming up, why they are getting together, and when the meeting will take place. You will want to hold a meeting or conference call to set the stage for an animated meeting, allow people to ask questions, and start the brainstorming process. Next, in the meeting or on the conference call, you will want to state the goal of the innovation storm so that everybody knows what they are getting themselves into. It is a good idea to have the guest facilitator introduce themselves in advance over a call, video conference, or in person to prepare the group for your big innovation day.

BRING THE TUNES

You will want to provide music to set the stage and have an upbeat environment using a Bluetooth speaker that fills the room. You should have awesome music playing before the meeting starts, during breaks in the middle of the meeting, and you can even play musical games such as Name that Tune. Towards the end of the book, we will discuss the prioritization and voting process during which you should play music as well; playing background music while people are voting adds to the environment. It's easy to create a fun environment with a good playlist and good music. *We recommend Spotify for a wide variety of music playlists and the Bose SoundLink Color portable speaker for sound.*

Let's get started…

"Today, if you're not disrupting yourself, someone else is; your fate is to be either the disrupter or the disrupted. There is no middle ground."
—Salim Ismail,
Author of Exponential Organizations

Ideas must be shared by all,
not just with all.

CHAPTER 1: PRE-STORM:
Agenda, Problem Statements, Growth Strategies

THE WELCOME

BEFORE EVERY INNOVATION storm, the leader of the organization should kick off the meeting with a formal introduction to the group. This can come from the owner of the business or leader of the business and should include an introduction of the facilitator. We also advise kicking off all meetings with an expression of gratitude, thanking the team for participating, summarizing of the goals for the day, and expressing excitement for the ideas coming out of the meeting. From this point forward, the facilitator is going to anchor and run the meeting, so after the introduction, the facilitator will specifically state the goals for the day, the reason why the idea storm has been so effective, and get the group ready to start.

NAMELESS AND RANK-LESS FEEDBACK

Now the facilitator will discuss the concept of nameless and rank-less feedback for all participants in the innovation storm. The positions or roles at the company of any participant of the day do not matter, and everybody should be able to provide ideas, solutions, and suggestions. It is the role of the facilitator to encourage everyone in the room to share and participate in the storm. This is one of the reasons why the manager or owner of the organization cannot be the facilitator. It is also important for the group to hold each other accountable. Any remarks that are heard or spoken, aloud or under the breath, that may be considered negative or "idea killers" should be called out. Do this by ringing the bell and throwing a BS flag at the person! The BS flags can be held by anyone and often change hands, and the person closest to the bell can be considered the negativity referee. If someone wants to volunteer for the role, let that person take over!

THE MINDSETS AND HOUSEKEEPING

After the introduction, there should be a clear review of the mindsets for the day and some housekeeping. For the mindsets of the day, see below. It is a good idea to write the mindsets on the whiteboard or on a separate easel for all to view. We will review the mindsets of the innovation storm below.

For housekeeping, it is important to make sure everyone is clear on where the restrooms are, discuss cellphone etiquette, and review the plan for breaks for the day. Let everyone know breaks will be taken throughout the day. The lunch plans should be determined and ordered ahead of time, and if intermittent bathroom breaks are needed, everyone should take them on their own. Otherwise, we will break every 1.5-2 hours.

A note on cellphone etiquette: The bullshit flag is great for throwing at people who are looking at their cell phone excessively, clearly writing an email, or texting too much. Throw the bullshit flag at them to call them out.

MINDSET #1

Be innovative, creative, and over the top. Leverage the absurd.

MINDSET #2

Don't agree.

MINDSET #3

Identify what's different about the problem, the approach, or the solution.

MINDSET #4

Force everyone to think. The environment and the chemistry are up to the group.

MINDSET #5

Engage everyone, ask deeper questions, and challenge assumptions.

MINDSET #6

Leave judgement at the door.

MINDSET #7

Listen differently. Eliminate already-always listening (thinking about your response while you listen to someone else speak).

MINDSET #8

Paraphrase and restate before we move on. All questions and ideas must be clearly defined and understood by all.

MINDSET #9

Diverse points of view are a gift. All feedback, angles of thought, and lenses in which we see the world are a gift to the entire group.

MINDSET #10

Holding back your thoughts is a lack of integrity.

If you are holding back your thoughts or views on the problems or ideas, then you are not expressing yourself fully. You are here today because you bring value to the entire organization. Simply put, if you are holding back, look internally as to why you feel you need to hold back. We value your thoughts and opinions, so please do not hold back.

Review the above mindsets out loud to the entire group and ensure everyone understands them. This is one of the first steps to opening creativity and setting the vibe for the day.

THE AGENDA FOR THE DAY

As the facilitator, you should have the summary agenda on the whiteboard, with no times listed for the day. The agenda is timeless because each portion of the agenda is critical and may take more or less time than anticipated. The agenda is more like a checklist for the day. Post the following agenda on the whiteboard, review each step, and explain briefly what each of the steps will look like. By posting this publicly, this will allow for members of the innovation storm to know exactly where we are in the day.

Here is the summary agenda to post on the whiteboard to review with the participants of the innovation storm:

The Pre Storm
Welcome & Introduction
Review Problem Statement
Review the four types of growth – decide on two for today
Question Storming
Refine the Scope
Summarize and Wrap Pre-Storm

The Storm
Introduction and Q&A – Format, Structure
Round 1 – Round Robin, One Each
Round 2 – Rapid Fire, Robust and Detailed, One Each, but as many turns as needed
Round 3 – Wrap Up with 10-second clarity on ideas

The Post-Storm
Ideas Have Alliances
Voting
4-6 Top Ideas
Prioritization: The Impact vs. Effort Matrix –
Let's get them in the goal zone
Long term: Identify the long-term opportunities
(those not in the goal zone)
Final Words from Leadership and Participants
Feedback and Thoughts
Rate the meeting: huddle and silly string
Adjourn

THE PRE-STORM: WE ALL GOT PROBLEMS

The goal of the pre-storm is to set the stage for creative brainstorming. The pre-storm is such a critical part of the day because it builds momentum. It is where we frame the structure of the day, get ideas flowing, and ultimately build chemistry as a group to step outside of the day-to-day operations of the organization and get in a mindset of disruptive thinking. Let's get going!

Prior to the pre-storm even starting, the main goal of the leadership team is to select a broad problem statement to address. A problem statement is the framework for an opportunity to arise during the innovation storm. The problem statement will be used to focus on one or two areas to grow the business. At times, organizations will host multiple innovation storms to attack multiple problem statements, sometimes as much as one per quarter.

A problem statement can be, and typically is, growth-based. However, it could be based around cost reduction, or a people/resources-based problem statement. A problem statement could also be grounded on innovating the brand or brand message of the organization.

A few broad stroke themes around your problem statement may include: ways to revolutionize the services of your organization, technology to add to the organization (consumer-facing or internal applications), evaluation and reorganization of the consumer buying process and consumer lifecycle, elimination of resources, branding changes, adding completely new services or products, and beyond.

Discovering an impactful problem statement is critical to the success of the innovation storm. To get you started, here are some questions from the book *Exponential Organizations* by Salim Ismail with a problem statement added to each.

- *Who is your customer?* How can we expand our reach?

- *Which customer problem are you solving?* What other problems can we solve?

- *What is your solution?* Does it improve the status quo by at least 10x?

- *How will you market the product or service?* What marketing innovations should we consider?

- *How are you selling the product or service?* What additional sales channels should we pursue?

- *How do you turn customers into advocates using viral effects and Net Promoter Scores to drive down the marginal cost of demand?*

- *How will you scale your customer segment?*

- *How will you drive the marginal cost of supply towards zero?* (This is one of the most disruptive questions we've seen— this is geared towards elimination.)

Here are a few more questions to consider before deciding on your problem statement (also see the appendix on example problem statements to get you started).

- What innovative marketing techniques can the organization utilize to improve sales?

- How can you modify your organization's products or services?

- What additional products or services can your organization offer?

- How do you deliver your brand?

- Do you need to make a brand change?

- Do we need to add roles and resources? New business areas or departments?

The problem statement should always be selected by the leadership team or owner of the organization and stated to the group ahead of time. It is a best practice to brainstorm your problem statement in a meeting or series of meetings. You may present two or three problem statements to your team ahead of time to spark creativity. We have come up with a list of problem statements to help you get started—they are listed in the appendix. You may use these exact statements, or use them to get your thoughts flowing.

Ninety percent of problem statements are in the form of a question and are geared at growth strategies for the organization. From the book *The Innovators Toolkit*, we know that when selecting a problem statement that involves a growth strategy, it is important to frame the innovation storm into a focus area of one or two growth opportunities. While an organization may want to attack all four growth strategies (which we will discuss next), it is a better practice to start with one or two at a time. Ideally, to dive deep into all four, you would want to hold at least two innovation storms.

Again, from the book *The Innovators Toolkit*, we know there are at least four different disruptive categories or growth strategies. Let's discuss what those different growth strategies are and how to apply them.

GROWTH STRATEGIES: HERE WE GROW AGAIN

Let's discuss four types of growth strategies for your innovation storm. These four growth strategies are discussed in the *Innovators Toolkit*, a book that was a huge inspiration for this guide, as mentioned above. The four types of growth strategies include:

- Core growth

- Related market growth

- Disruptive growth

- New market growth

CORE GROWTH

This type of growth will add to your existing business. This can be done by bringing better solutions to the organization and providing clients with improved services or products. This involves innovation and improvement of your current products or services. Core growth can even apply to marketing innovation in the way we acquire clients or sell products. Simply put, core growth is changing or adding to the existing business model.

RELATED MARKET GROWTH

Related market growth involves taking an existing customer base and providing new solutions. These are new products or services that relate to your core business, but will be attractive or needed by your existing client base. The related market is not about improving what you currently have, but about adding new solutions to your existing customer base.

DISRUPTIVE GROWTH

Disruptive growth typically involves approaching your market, or similar markets, with an innovative method to the way the service or product is delivered. This could mean altering a product so much that it significantly changes an entire industry or the way the product or service is consumed. Many times, disruptive change involves lowering the barriers to entry for the consumer, thus significantly lowering the time and/or cost of consuming the service or product. Think about Airbnb and Uber and the impact they've had on their perspective markets.

Disruptive growth is achieved often when outsiders enter an industry or market and ask why, or why not, and then push ancient beliefs and systems to improve. Ultimately, you end up with different business models, attracting a different buyer into an industry that has evolved to support this new disruptive technology, product, service, or marketing technique. When we say, "the next big thing," we usually are describing disruptive growth.

NEW MARKET GROWTH

New market growth involves doing something completely new to attract an entirely new set of customers and users. It could be a new service offering, a new product line, a new brand, or starting a new organization with new solutions for the market you are going to be entering.

ENOUGH WITH THE STRATEGY, LET'S GET STARTED:

By now you have educated your leadership team on the goals of the innovation storm, you've discussed growth strategies and problem statements, and you've educated your innovation storm attendees on the growth strategy you will focus on, as well as the problem statement(s) that you will be addressing. Your problem statements need to be vague and open. You want to capture the imagination of the team and leave plenty of room for interpretation and inventiveness. Creativity and origination requires space to develop and flourish. Now let's use a technique called the question invasion to get the entire group in the creative mindset.

"Failure is an option here. If things are not failing, you are not innovating enough."
—Elon Musk

QUESTION INVASION

The question invasion stage of the innovation storm is setting the stage for the entire day. This is where creativity, innovation, pure guts (because we are going to see who has the guts to ask the hard questions), and entertainment will get started. The rules of the question invasion portion of the pre-storm are just simply to ask questions, and only questions. Non-questions get a BS flag thrown or a bell rung.

During the question invasion session, the facilitator and one or two volunteers should be writing down the questions on the board. Depending on the size of the group, you may want to ask two volunteers to write on the board and the facilitator can focus on keeping the questions flowing.

Questions should come in all forms, be clearly stated, and written on the whiteboard or easel boards. They should ask who, what, when, where, and why. Here are some examples of great disruptive questions:

- Why do we need doctors?
- Why do we need cars?
- Does _____ department need to exist?
- What happens if we go directly to the front-line staff?
- Do we need brick and mortar locations?
- Why do we do this?
- What happens if we do this?
- What can we eliminate from this process?

By asking random questions, and getting the entire room asking questions, we are setting the stage for nameless and rank-less feedback, and getting everyone in the room to contribute. Not all the participants are going to be comfortable with public speaking or sharing their ideas, so the purpose of the question invasion is two-fold: to stretch our creative minds by only asking questions, and to inspire everyone to participate by building a comfort level for the upcoming innovation storm.

If you are the facilitator, you want to encourage questions that will disrupt industry, services, and products. What complaints or suggestions have team members overheard from clients, customers, employees, or each other? Encourage the team to think about complaints they've heard or read online about their service or industry. Convert those complaints into real questions and ideas for how to fix them. A strong facilitator is going to remind team members to challenge the status quo about any part of the organization.

The questioning session is the first portion of the day where opportunities will start to surface. Some participants will be so creative they will phrase their idea in the form of a question, or their question will lead the group to have an "aha" moment when they realize an opportunity was just posed in the form of a question. The questioning session creates the passion, collaboration, and momentum that will set the stage for the innovation storm. Do not speed through the invasion—make sure you write down all questions, encourage all team members to contribute, and ask tough questions. Tough questions disrupt businesses, challenge entire departments, transformation industries, and change the world. Now is the time to bring all opinions to the surface, get them out in the form of a question, and get our imaginative thoughts on the board.

Simple rules for the question storming portion of the day are:

1. Questions only.

2. No negative reactions or responses.

3. Questions only.

The bell and the BS flag are in the room to be rung and/or a flag thrown at someone who speaks without asking a question and/or makes a negative comment. *Use these tools.*

After all questions have been written on a whiteboard, take photos of the questions for future reference. After the question invasion, break the room for 15 minutes, take photos of your questions, and clear the board for the innovation storm. Now let's move on to the next step!

"Sometimes it takes outsiders to look at an industry and say, hey, this is broken, or this isn't working and to come in and disrupt it."
—Neil Blumenthal,
Co-Founder, Warby Parker

If a team isn't growing together, it is most certainly growing apart.

CHAPTER 2: PRE-STORM:
Defining The Scope Of Work

B EFORE WE END our pre-storm, and in preparation for the innovation storm, it is critical to define the scope of work of the organization. This is the job statement—defining exactly what the organization does. This is a great team-building and cohesion exercise that asks team members to reflect on and define what exactly the organization does, how the organization delivers that to their client base, and what can go wrong in the delivery process or in the consumption of the products or services the organization provides. We will also consider what barriers to entry the consumer may encounter along the buyer's lifecycle.

WHAT DO YOU DO?

The first step in defining the scope of work is to define exactly what it is that the organization does. Not theory, not some fancy definition or mission statement, but let's say exactly what the organization does or produces. The first step is to write down, in the middle of a large notepad or whiteboard, exactly what the organization does. *Make sure it is in the middle of the board because we are going to write statements above and below this scope of work statement. See the illustration above.*

WHY DO YOUR CLIENTS PURCHASE YOUR PRODUCTS OR SERVICES?

After you have defined exactly what it is your organization does, you are going to record all the reasons why your clients utilize your products or services. Above the scope of work that you recorded in the middle of the whiteboard or easel pad, you are going to ask your team, "Why does the consumer utilize our services or products?" Your goal is to record all the reasons why people utilize your organization. Encourage team members to think outside the box here and not just list the obvious answers. Ask the team, "Why do consumers really utilize our products or services?"

Here are some examples of digging deeper into the questions "what we do" and "why consumers use our products or services": *(use these to spark creativity within the group)*

- Starbucks coffee: because it is good coffee or because the client needs a place to work for the morning – Does the coffee customer need temporary office space?

- Junk removal: to clean out the garage – Do we sell junk removal services, or do we sell space and time?

32

- Spotify Streaming Music: $10 for unlimited music per month, or $10 for therapy and escape from the daily grind?

- A new pair of running shoes: Just new running shoes, or hopes and dreams as the runner sets new goals and a new journey towards health and fitness?

Spend time with your team exploring exactly what it is your organization does, what exactly you provide your end user, and why they utilize your products or services. This exercise has proven to be a strong team-building event, as well as helping bring teams closer to disruption and creative thinking mindsets.

WHAT ARE THE BARRIERS FOR THE CONSUMER? WHAT CAN GO WRONG?

After you define the scope of work and state exactly why your clients consume your products or services, the final step is to express what issues can arise in the transfer or the consumption of your products or services. The statements and issues that are collected for this will be recorded underneath the scope of work statement.

To define the issues that consumers may encounter during the entire lifecycle of being a client of your organization, you want to ask your team members to list all the issues that can occur. Think as minor or as major as possible.

Here are some questions to get your team started:

- What are the most common complaints?

- What are the rare complaints?

- What are the issues that could happen?

- What can go wrong before your client becomes a client?

- What can go wrong after they become a client?

- What are the barriers to achieving 100% customer satisfaction?

- What are the most common reasons clients do not score your products or services a 100% or a 10 out of 10?

- Why would they choose to utilize a competitor instead of your organization?

- Why would a potential client decide not to purchase or utilize your services or that of your competitors at all?

Put these answers on the whiteboard under the scope of work and make sure to get them all down. Take your time during this exercise, as this is the last step in discovering and warming up the creative minds of your team.

By now you have defined your scope of work, you've discussed "the why" behind why a client becomes a part of your organization, and you have ended this session with a deep dive into what exactly can go wrong within the lifecycle of your client. All three of these exercises have stretched the creativity of your team as you have explored what is it you do, why your clients use your product or services, and what can go wrong. You have also executed a questioning session around the who, what, when, where, and why and challenged each other to go deeper into these opportunities. Ideas are flowing, thoughts are coming to fruition, teams are taking notes, and now it is time to hold the innovation storm and get all the ideas on the whiteboard!! Now is a great time for the facilitator to ask the group to take a 10-minute stretch break and get ready to dive into the main part of the day—the innovation storm!

"If you want to create a great product, just focus on one person. Make that one person have the most amazing experience ever."
—Brian Chesky, Co-Founder, Airbnb

CHAPTER 3:
The Innovation Storm

Y OU HAVE WORKED hard with the team, opening lines of communication, stretching creativity, expressing and exercising nameless and rank-less feedback, and some hard questions have been asked. Just like a great pre-game warm-up, the team is ready for game time. Let's get started.

Remember, you have selected one or two growth strategies and narrowed down your problem statement. During the day, you may find an opportunity to do another innovation storm with a different focus. For example, in the franchising industry, a franchisor delivers franchisee support and end-user customer experience, both of which could support multiple innovation storms per year.

It is time for the main event. Restroom and snack breaks should have been taken, music should be playing, the energy levels are up, and the entire team now feels the chemistry in the room. We are warmed up and ready to play. Let's get some ideas flowing.

FLOWING IDEAS & CHALLENGING QUESTIONS

Welcome everyone back in the room. Cut the music, and let's get started. The first round of the innovation storm will be round robin style and each person will share one idea. It doesn't have to be their "best" idea because everyone will get plenty of opportunities to share, but we will start with one idea. To start, go around the room, and ask everyone to share. First, ask someone to volunteer to start. That will start the innovation storm, and the group will go clockwise starting with that person, then the following person, and so on. By now the storm kit should be in full force. Bells should be out (the bell and the BS flag are for any negative responses), and markers should be given to every person in the room. Ideas should be flowing and writing should be happening.

The role of the facilitator is not just to keep the meeting moving, but to keep ideas flowing. To do so, you must have an arsenal of questions to get the team thinking and keep creativity brewing... The following list of questions will spark ideas, encourage bold sharing, and ensure a list of business improvements are explored in any one-day innovation storm. *The facilitator should put these questions on index cards and keep those cards by their side.*

Challenging questions to get any meeting flowing:

✓ What can we substitute an alternative solution for?

✓ Where do we need to add a feature?

✓ What can we eliminate?

✓ What can we combine?

✓ What in the organization needs to be modified?

✓ What are our customers not happy with?

✓ What are our customers asking for?

✓ What are our competitors doing that we aren't? What are other industries doing that we need to do?

✓ Can we do something cheaper?

✓ Is there something we can do and charge a premium for?

✓ What options are our customers asking for?

✓ Is there a process we can rearrange to be more efficient?

✓ What training or education do our customers need more of? Our team members?

✓ How can we leverage the absurd to create the powerful?

✓ Leave budget, time, resources, and people out of your equation… What's next? What's possible?

✓ Think big!! In your wildest dreams, where can this business go? What will be needed to get us there?

The facilitator can shout out loud: *"THINK BIG. DREAM BIG. THINK FANTASY LAND IN YOUR BUSINESS. WHERE ARE WE GOING?"*

When a participant calls out their idea, the facilitator's role is to first clarify the idea or validate that the idea makes sense and is clear to everyone in the room. Once the idea has been precisely stated, the facilitator will ask the person to write the idea down clearly on the sticky note, and turn it in to the facilitator or a volunteer that is helping to collect the ideas. Then stick the ideas on the wall in no certain order (at least not yet.) *See the photos for examples.* Once you have gone full circle and everyone has shared one example, it is time for a round of quick fire.

Quick fire is exactly what it sounds like. This is the opportunity for participants to rapid fire their ideas. One at a time, team members will shout out ideas. You still want to emphasize that the ideas must be clear and understood by all, but this round will move at a faster pace. Do this rapid fire round as much as needed; if ideas are flowing, keep the round going.

As the room starts to slow down with ideas, we will wrap up the main innovation storm with one final round of quick ideas where each person has up to 15 seconds to state and refine their idea. Then it must be put on the board. As the energy and creativity begin to wind down, and ideas are less frequent, the facilitator should make sure to leave time for last-minute ideas. Do not rush the end of the session; rather, ask the team a few times if there are any other ideas—leave room for any last-minute thoughts.

After all the ideas are out and they all have been clearly defined, written on sticky notes, and are all posted to the wall, you should have a multi-colored wall with a ton of ideas. *When using multi-color sticky notes, you do not need to try to identify a category for each color. Just put them on the wall and we will categorize shortly after.*

After you wrap up the innovation storm main event, take a 10-minute break to categorize. As the facilitator, before you break the room, ask for two to four volunteers to help you categorize the ideas. The volunteers must know the business well, as they will help advise on which ideas go in which category, and assist in naming each category. Once you have your two to four volunteers, break the room for 10 minutes and then get categorizing.

"Move fast and break things.
Unless you are breaking stuff,
you are not moving fast enough."
—Mark Zuckerberg, Facebook

A leader is responsible for creating an environment where ideas can thrive.

CHAPTER 4:
Post-Storm

IDEAS DESERVE A FAMILY

Now that you have finished your innovation storm, and while the participants are on their break, you should have at least two volunteers and numerous ideas on the wall. It is time to organize them into families (aka, categories) before you vote on the ideas for prioritization. The goal of grouping is to have three categories to place the ideas in. Once all ideas have been categorized, we will start voting and the prioritization process. Grouping takes place while many of the participants are on a 10-minute break.

At minimum, the facilitator and two volunteers who are close to the business should start reading the ideas to themselves. All ideas should be read and reviewed by the volunteers and the facilitator. Patterns should start to develop.

If you see patterns in the form of a category for your ideas, write the potential category on top of the whiteboard or on a separate easel. You will develop your own categories as you are grouping your ideas, but here are some examples to use:

- ✓ Technology
- ✓ Services

✓ Products

✓ App (maybe a ton of ideas came out about a new app)

✓ Changes to existing services/products

✓ People/Resources

✓ Misc.

Before you finalize your three categories, you want to also check your ideas for duplicates, similarities, or ideas you can combine to make one larger idea. You will want to take the sticky notes for these ideas that are combined or are duplicates of each other and place them next to each other, and categorize them as one idea. This will reduce the number of ideas you have, but having multiple sticky notes for one idea will be a visual to the group that the idea is popular and was presented more than once.

Once you have decided on three categories, write them at the top of your large whiteboard, or give each category its own individual easel pad. You should leave lots of room horizontally, and make sure each column for each category is at least 24 inches wide—this is where the ideas will be placed and where voting will take place. *See photo for a better understanding.* The facilitator and the volunteers should be placing each idea in its perspective category, stacked vertically in one column per category, as voting will take place next to each sticky note.

Now you are ready to get started. Participants should be heading back into the room to get settled. It's time to vote! But first, let's explain the categories and the voting process to the team.

> *"Your ideas are all great; I love them all,*
> *now just tell me where to get started."*
> *—Joe Bourdow, Former President,*
> *ValPak, in an address to a newly formed*
> *Franchise Advisory Council.*

I DECLARE A VOTE

At this point of the day you have your ideas on the whiteboard or easel pads in the form of one idea per sticky note. It is time to vote, but first you must share the categories with your group. Start by thanking the volunteers who helped to create the categories and ensure all the ideas are aligned. These volunteers served a huge part of the day, and we want to make sure to thank them for their hard work.

Now the facilitator will share aloud to the entire group the three categories that were chosen. The facilitator should explain to the group that the categories were created so we all have multiple votes per person, per category. The goal is to prioritize and come out of the voting with at least six high-priority ideas. Lastly, we will rank the ideas based on feasibility, but first let's vote.

To vote, we first will go back in time… A time when we were sitting in grade school, when we had to sound out numbers around the room so we could break the room into three groups for voting purposes. This will ensure the front of the room is not a chaos-driven frenzy geared towards the best ideas. Here is the step-by-step process on how to get the voting started:

Step 1: In a round robin style format, have each person go around the room and sound out their number. Start with the person closest to the facilitator and assign them 1, the next person clockwise 2, then 3, then back to 1, then 2, then 3. Each person should be going around the room going 1, 2, 3…1, 2, 3…1, 2, 3…1, 2, 3. *Remind them to remember their numbers or write it down on a sticky note.*

Step 2: Above each category, assign it a number by writing that number in a box, nice and bold.

Step 3: Assign the number of votes. THIS IS AN IMPORTANT FORMULA. To assign the number of votes each person gets to have per category, take the total number of ideas and divide by three (TOTAL # OF IDEAS/3. This equals the number of votes per person, per category.

Example: 100 ideas/5 – 20 votes per person per category.

Question: Can I use multiple votes per idea?

Answer: Yes, but there is a catch! Only 25% of your votes can go to one idea. If you have 20 votes per category, then up to five votes can be applied to one idea.

Now that you have read this step, you should be envisioning the craziness that is about to follow. You'll need lots of room at the front of your room to allow people to move around, and your ideas and category columns need to be big enough with enough space in between each other to allow for people to vote. Make sure you have plenty of room. Even consider using different rooms or different walls so your participants have enough room to move around.

To vote, each participant will make a check mark next to their idea. Remind the group they can use up to 25% of their total votes per category on one idea. They must keep track of the number of votes they've used on their own, as we are using the honor system. *No lobbying of ideas can take place at the boards.* Allow participants to make their own decisions.

YOU'VE GOT SOME WINNERS, NOW WHAT?

Now that all your ideas are categorized and you've executed a team vote, it is time to review and select ideas put into action. We will also identify long-term initiatives. This is done by holding an impact vs. effort debate. We will go in depth into what the impact vs. effort debate is in the next paragraph. The goals are to place each winning idea on a matrix after a team discussion to determine the feasibility of each idea. Let's get started.

After all rounds of voting, we should have some clear winners in each category. You will have one or two clear winners that come in near each other in total votes. The facilitator should first define the clear winners and circle them to visually declare them as the winners. This does not mean the other ideas won't be taken into consideration (all ideas will be recorded and published for future reference), but the winners will be discussed in our impact vs. effort matrix.

The impact vs. effort matrix is a visual tool used to determine which of your winning ideas should be executed and when. It is a tool that will allow for open discussion about each idea and potential owners of the implementation phase. All stakeholders and those responsible for executing the ideas should be in discussions about the time, resources, and investment required to execute each idea. This is the first step in implementation.

On the effort vs. impact matrix, the X axis is titled "Effort" and the Y axis is titled "Impact." Each axis will have a scale of 1-10 from left to right. For the effort scale, 1 is easiest to execute, create, or implement, and 10 will be the most difficult to execute, create, or implement. For impact, 1 will be least impactful, and 10 being most impactful (in comparison to the other winning ideas).

The facilitator should identify the top winning idea (number of total votes) and start the discussion. Ask the room to discuss where this is on an impact and effort scale of 1-10, and discuss where to place it on the matrix.

Once everyone agrees on the score for the idea and where it belongs on the matrix, re-write the idea and place it on the matrix. Continue this for all ideas until the entire group has agreed on where each idea falls on the impact vs. effort matrix.

Remember that each idea is in comparison to the other winning ideas, so it is completely normal to debate these, and the group may change their mind while trying to place them on the matrix. That is acceptable, and healthy debate is encouraged.

THE SWEET SPOT: EFFORT VS. IMPACT

Congratulations, you are officially at the end of the one-day innovation storm! You have successfully set the stage for creativity, hosted an awesome event, gathered ideas from around your company, built culture, and strengthened your team cohesion. I know you've found ideas that will propel your organization to the next level and raise the bar for your market and competitors.

The last thing the facilitator did with the team was place the top six to eight ideas on the impact vs. effort matrix. The "sweet" spot for this matrix is the top left quadrant (if the matrix were divided into four quadrants). The top left quadrant is the highly impactful ideas that are less than a 5 to implement on the scale of 1-10 of difficulty. The ideas that end up in this "sweet" spot are either going to be quick wins that someone can own and begin execution on the day of the meeting, or they can be quarterly initiatives, also known as "rocks." Rocks are quarterly or annual initiatives introduced in the book *Traction* by Gino Wickman.

IMPORTANT: *Implementation is the vital key to ensuring the time and resource investment you've made in the innovation storm was a valuable one. It is easy to end the day on a high note, but it is so important to spend time to discuss implementation. Please make sure you do not skip over the communication of who takes ownership of the ideas and who will be responsible to implement or execute them by when.*

What about the other winning ideas, those that made it to the effort vs. impact matrix? Great question… for the ideas that made it on the high impact scale, but which are also highly difficult to implement due to time, resources, cash, technology, or another reason are still great ideas. These ideas become annual initiatives, three-year plans, long-term vision items, b-hag (big hairy audacious goals), or investment projects where specific teams will need to be created or assigned.

These are the huge opportunities that require follow-up meetings to discuss feasibility, cost, timelines, project management strategies, and more. The leadership team should be recording these impactful opportunities and plan discussions around execution of these in quarterly and annual planning sessions.

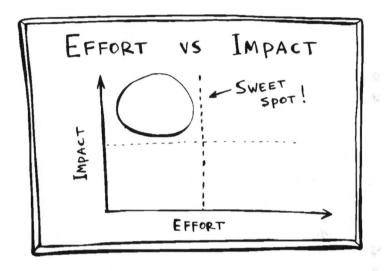

COLLECT, PROCESS, AND WRAP THE DAY

It's time to break the room for the day. First, the facilitator should thank everyone for participating, and thank them for allowing you to facilitate such an awesome day. The facilitator should then ask the leadership team to say a few parting words about the team building and culture that took place for the day and about the ideas that came out of the day. The facilitator should remind the team to keep the ideas in mind and that the ideas and questions asked will be published for future reference. They are great to pull out in quarterly planning sessions and to share with team members who were unable to attend.

Once the attendees have left the room, make sure to take clear photos of all the ideas, the categories, and the impact vs. effort matrix. It is a best practice to utilize a freelancer from Fiverr.com or Upwork.com to transcribe the photos of the questions and ideas onto a document. The facilitator can then take this document and share it and save it within the organization for future use.

Ask those closest to the front lines
what they need and what does
the customer need.

BONUS:
Implementation
-Ideas must be adhesive

CONGRATULATIONS ON FINISHING Part 1 of this book which explained how to hold an innovation storm and disrupt from within. This day will change your company's future and help guide your next quarterly or annual planning session. The ideas and projects to come from this meeting will launch your organization further, and your team members will have buy-in—especially when they get to see, or better yet work on, projects they came up with, or were a part of when it was just in infancy. You will have disrupted your organization from within, and your team will appreciate you for doing so.

If you have not done so, your next read will need to be *Traction* by Gino Wickman. In *Traction*, you will learn tools and meeting rhythms to hold teams accountable, execute effective annual planning retreats and quarterly meetings, and communicate to your front lines effectively. If you take the strongest ideas and run with them, and implement the systems in *Traction* in your organization, you will have an incredibly disruptive year, as well as a whole new organization. Your teams will see and feel the momentum you have built. The perfect formula for a disruptive year is implementing *Traction* and holding your one-day innovation storm at least once annually.

Finally, my last piece of advice is to not hold bad meetings. You should see by now the innovation storm is fun, creative, all-encompassing, and has an agenda. You should feel empathy for anyone that attends your meetings, thus making them fun, impactful, and meaningful. Don't waste time and do not waste the creative energy of anyone who does not have to be there, just because you feel they should. To check your meeting style, ensure your meetings are appropriate and effective (and a bit fun as well), check out Cameron Herold's book, *Meetings Suck*. It will help you!

You are ready to host your innovation storm and disrupt your organization from within. When seeking inspiration, or wondering why seek out ideas, remember a few things from the book *Origins* by Adam Grant. Picasso drew thousands of pieces to come up with a masterpiece. Beethoven and Bach both wrote over 600 pieces of music each but are only known as legends for a few great compositions. Shakespeare wrote 37 plays and over 150 sonnets but is only known for a few... now go generate ideas and find your masterpiece.

Justin Waltz is available for live facilitation of innovation sessions, quarterly planning sessions, and organizational annual planning retreats. To inquire please email JW@JustinWaltz.com.

"Every year, take everything out of your strategic plan. Make everything fight its way back into the plan – every year."
—Troy Hazard

Creativity takes time.
Don't rush the process.

BONUS:
Destroy your one-page plan annually

I F YOU LOVED the innovation storm and are in the mindset of disruption, it is a great idea to disrupt your one-year strategic plan or three-year vision, at every annual planning session. Do not overthink this idea—simply take your strategic plan, break it down into action items and the ideas you wrote down with the team one year prior, and list them on a whiteboard or an easel. This same process applies for a three-year vision and ten-year b-hag (big hairy audacious goal). As a facilitator and for graphical effect, strike a line through each strategic plan item.

The next steps are as a group—using the same mindsets and rules during the innovation storm, debate and discuss the impact vs. effort of each item on the strategic plan.

Here are questions to get you started:

✓ What has the team learned since the strategic plan or vision was developed?

✓ What still makes sense?

✓ What needs to be modified?

✓ What needs to be eliminated?

✓ What is no longer relevant?

✓ What is completed and was celebrated?

✓ What should be added?

✓ How has the industry or business changed and how does that need to be reflected in our one-page plan or long-term vision?

Once debated, circle or re-write the items that remain, items that were reworded or rewritten, and new items on another whiteboard or easel. Then begin to recraft your revised and updated one-page strategic plan. This is an efficient and impactful method to ensure your strategic plan is updated and revised as the organization changes and adapts. Now get to work!

APPENDIX:
Innovation Storm
Problem Statements

1. How can we deliver a better experience to our customer?

2. What can we add to our customer service experience to enhance their experience?

3. How can we reduce our customer pipeline to shorten the customer cycle from need to end user?

4. What disruptive technology can we add to our service model?

5. What products are our customers asking for that they are currently not getting?

6. What innovative ways can we improve our client experience when they enter our brand?

7. What innovative ways can we increase lead flow?

8. What innovation can we bring to our marketing efforts?

9. What new solutions can we bring to our existing customers that have already done business with us?

10. What other markets should we enter into that align with our core business?

11. What ancillary services can we offer to our clients?

12. What products can we produce that will invite new clients into our business?

13. How can we change our product or service to disrupt the market at a lower price point?

14. What premium products or services can we add to offer our existing clients to increase our price or add a new level of product or service?

15. What solutions are our clients asking for that we should offer?

16. What solutions are our non-clients asking for that would get us into markets we currently do not exist in?

17. If our customers spoke to us, what would they say?

18. What have you learned from our customers lately that needs to be reported?

19. What brand innovations do we need to make an impact on our market?

20. What disruptive changes to our business model will we need to make in the next 5-10 and 50 years to uplift our market?

APPENDIX:
Innovation Storm
Optional Supplies

PAPER AIRPLANE KITS:

https://www.amazon.com/Kangaroos-Paper-Airplane-Kit-Airplanes/dp/B01LX8XY7V/ref=sr_1_13?ie=UT-F8&qid=1499366779&sr=8-13&keywords=paper+planes

FIDGET SPINNER:

https://www.amazon.com/Fidget-Spinner-Killer-Siliver-White/dp/B06Y4J6K2D/ref=sr_1_22?rps=1&ie=UT-F8&qid=1499366874&sr=8-22&keywords=Fidget+Spinner&refin-ements=p_85%3A2470955011

https://www.amazon.com/Fidget-Spinner-Toy-Time-Killer/dp/B06ZZMSJ59/ref=pd_sim_21_3?_encoding=UTF8&pd_rd_i=B06ZZMSJ59&pd_rd_r=J8DC6MRKDRB9MYR2H2PK&pd_rd_w=Ew0tE&pd_rd_wg=7OdOV&psc=1&refRID=J8DC6MRK-DRB9MYR2H2PK

STICKY NOTES:

https://www.amazon.com/Post-Inches-Collection-Notes-654-8AN/dp/B00NPANTZ0/ref=sr_1_6?s=office-products&ie=UTF8&qid=1499370745&sr=1-6&keywords=post+it+notes

DRY ERASE MARKERS:

https://www.amazon.com/Low-Odor-Markers-Chisel-16-Pack-Assorted/dp/B000J09OLM/ref=sr_1_5?s=office-products&ie=UTF8&qid=1499370811&sr=1-5&keywords=whiteboard+markers

SHARPIE MARKERS THIN:

https://www.amazon.com/Sharpie-Permanent-Markers-Assorted-32893PP/dp/B0003WN0CA/ref=sr_1_2?s=office-products&ie=UTF8&qid=1499370849&sr=1-2&keywords=sharpie+markers+thin

SILLY STRING:

https://www.amazon.com/SILLY-Crazy-Party-STRING-can/dp/B005FC8SX4/ref=sr_1_cc_7?s=aps&ie=UTF8&qid=1499370949&sr=1-7-catcorr&keywords=silly+string

PLAY DOH:

https://www.amazon.com/Play-Doh-10-Pack-Colors-Amazon-Exclusive/dp/B00JM5GW10/ref=sr_1_1?s=toys-and-games&ie=UTF8&qid=1499370983&sr=1-1-spons&keywords=play%2Bdoh&th=1

PIPE CLEANERS:

https://www.amazon.com/Creativity-Street-Chenille-150-Count-Assorted/dp/B00A6VWMYK/ref=sr_1_9?s=toys-and-games&ie=UTF8&qid=1499371059&sr=1-9&keywords=pipe+cleaners

ALUMINUM FLIP CHART:

https://www.amazon.com/Lightweight-Aluminum-Flip-Chart-Presentation-Inches/dp/B0042AUMTS/ref=pd_bxgy_201_img_2?_encoding=UTF8&pd_rd_i=B0042AUMTS&pd_rd_r=ZR41M0YPM8958V3BP66K&pd_rd_w=ZZnDK&pd_rd_wg=EGR7N&psc=1&refRID=ZR41M0YPM8958V3BP66K

STICKY EASEL PAD:

https://www.amazon.com/Post-Self-Stick-Easel-Inches-30-Sheet/dp/B00006IA9F/ref=pd_bxgy_229_img_2?_encoding=UTF8&pd_rd_i=B00006IA9F&pd_rd_r=CMQGSR72K0831VTSSJ8E&pd_rd_w=vJWdC&pd_rd_wg=MTrhL&psc=1&refRID=CMQGS-R72K0831VTSSJ8E

BS FLAG:

https://www.amazon.com/BS-Industries-Bullshit-Flag-Uncensored/dp/B005KKAWQC

BELL:

https://www.amazon.com/Advantus-Diameter-Brushed-Nickel-CB10000/dp/B0013CQFZS/ref=sr_1_3?ie=UTF8&qid=1499371302&sr=8-3&keywords=bell

APPENDIX:
One-Day Innovation Storm Facilitators Guide

With Sample Agenda & Notes
(for facilitator use)

NOTE: NO TIMES ARE PROVIDED; ESTIMATED TIME TO COMPLETE (DEPENDING ON SIZE OF TEAM) IS 3-5 HOURS.

Hold a pre-call with leadersion prior to the storm, ideally three to four weeks in advance. All attendee calls should be one week in advance. Here is what you should cover:

- *<u>With Leadership</u>: Discussion points: Structure, attendees, the space/room, decide on a Problem Statement.*

- *<u>With Attendees</u>: Discussion points: Facilitator will introduce himself/herself. Share the why, what it is, the Problem Statement that has been set, the structure and the agenda, share what nameless and rank-less feedback means, expectations, housekeeping/logistics, and open to Q&A.*

<u>Summary Agenda</u>

THE PRE-STORM

Welcome & Introduction

Review Problem Statement

Review the four types of growth – decide on two for today

Question Storming

Refine the Scope

Summarize and Wrap

THE STORM

Introduction and Q&A – Review format and structure

Round 1 – Round robin, one per attendee

Round 2 – Rapid fire, robust and detailed, as many turns as needed

Round 3 – Wrap up with 15-second clarity on ideas

THE POST-STORM

Grouping

Voting

4-6 Top Ideas

Prioritization: The Impact vs. Effort Matrix — Let's get them in the goal zone

Long term: Identify the long-term opportunities (those not in the goal zone)

Final words from leadership and participants: feedback and thoughts

Rate the meeting

Adjourn

The Facilitator Guide for the Day of the Storm

THE PRE-STORM
WELCOME & INTRODUCTION

I. Facilitator BEFORE guests arrive – make sure room is prepped, whiteboards clean, markers ready, toys on the tables (Sticky notes, BS flag, bells, silly string, pipe cleaners, fidget spinners, playdoh, etc.)

    Tip: Write agenda on whiteboards or pads so guests can follow along. Also write the problem statement(s) on the boards or pads.

II. Introduction from the founder, leader, or promoter of the storm – discuss the goals for the day, team-building activity, nameless and rank-less feedback, general introduction to the problem statement, and introduce the facilitator.

III. Introducer sits down. Facilitator takes over.

IV. Discuss the structure; describe nameless, rank-less feedback and the purpose of this; describe the rules and the purpose of the toys on the table.

V. Go over any housekeeping, timeliness of breaks (it's up to the facilitator to break the room when people get antsy and ready), restrooms, beverages, etc. Allow any questions for housekeeping.

VI. Review the agenda in detail so everyone has an idea of what the day is going to look like and how it will flow. Now you are ready to get started.

PRE-STORM

I. Review the broad problem statement(s) with the entire team.

II. Ask: *Does everyone clearly understand the problem statement? Is it a broad statement? (That is a good thing.) Do we understand the opportunity? Can we add to it?*

III. What is the growth strategy we are seeking? Review each type of growth and discuss the one or two growth strategies we are seeking.

    a. Core Growth

    b. Related Market Growth

    c. Disruptive Growth

    d. New Market Growth

QUESTION STORMING SESSION

I. Explain the WHY: We are going to ask questions about our problem statement – these can be ridiculous questions, they can challenge what we are already doing, they can challenge why we haven't progressed, they can challenge reality or science, they can open our minds to new opportunity. No question is a bad question.

II. Additional material for explaining the WHY: By asking questions in regard to our organization, our services, our customers, our products, our technology, our personnel, our systems, etc., we open up our minds and begin to enter a creative space. As a group, we are now creating chemistry to open up our thoughts to endless possibility and big opportunity. This is all part of the process.

III. Remind the group one more time that no one can answer a question or make a general statement or a statement about a question. The rules of this part of the Pre-Storm are for questions only.

IV. Now that you have everyone ready, it's time to question storm for at least 20-30 minutes; maybe longer. Ask for one volunteer if you have under 10 participants; two volunteers if you have more than 10 total participants.

V. Explain to your volunteers they are to record questions for a total of 10 minutes and then you will ask for new volunteers. Have them record each question exactly. Once they are ready, it's time to get started.

VI. Ask the group to get started – spitball questions to your volunteers; they should be recording questions on your whiteboard or your pads.

VII. When 10 minutes is up, ask for two more volunteers and switch out the question storm writers so the original writers can provide questions.

VIII. Encourage the group, give positive reinforcement like, "That's great," "Love it," "Awesome," "Let's keep going." Ask questions such as, "Does make sense to all; do we need to clarify that at all?"

IX. Once the questions start to slow down, do a final round robin roll call and ask each participant to add one more question or pass if they feel they have said all they have.

X. Now you have completed the question storming session.

Break the room for 10 minutes!

Time to Refine the Scope of our Job – What exactly is it that we do?

I. First write on whiteboard – *What is the job we do?* Allow the team to answer, and write all answers up on the whiteboard.

II. *Why do consumers get this job done?* Again, allow the team to answer, and write all answers up on the whiteboard.

III. *What are the narrower issues? What are barriers to getting the job done? What issues arise that prevent the job from happening or happening well?* Again, write these down.

IV. Now we have completed the scope of our job, it's time to recap and wrap up the Pre-Storm. Ideas should be flowing now!

WRAP UP THE PRE-STORM

I. Summarize by telling the team we just defined our Problem Statement, stretched our imagination with a Question Storming session, and defined the Scope of our Job.

II. Congratulate the team on a great prep session, and tell them it's now time for the core part of the day! We prepped our minds and are in a great creative space… Let's get started!

Break the room for 10 minutes!

THE STORM
IDEA STORMING – LET'S GET STARTED

I. Welcome everyone back in the room.

II. By now, everyone should have been writing down ideas as they came to mind, and if they had a marker and a stack of sticky notes in front of them, they will have already written them down on a sticky note.

III. Round 1 – Round Robin: We start with one person and we go around the room; clockwise or counter, it does not matter. Each person shares ONE idea and only one for now.

IV. Facilitator – Repeat the idea; ask the room, "Is that clear? Does anyone need clarity?"

V. Once all parties agree the idea is clear, ask the idea author to record it on the sticky note and hand it to you (facilitator) – *Tip: You may want assistance in gathering the ideas so you are not trying to run around the room and facilitate the idea storming.*

VI. Round 2 – You've completed a full rotation. Now open the room to one idea per person but rapid fire. Make sure to do the above and get clarity on each idea. **Stick them all up on the wall.**

VII. Round 3 – Your rapid-fire round should be the most robust, and by now the ideas are starting to trickle down.

VIII. Do one final round of idea storming. All ideas must be clarified in 15 seconds or less, to wrap up the idea storming of the session but allow for more ideas to flow.

IX. Congratulate the room on the awesome idea storming they just did – thank them and give a round of applause.

X. Let the group know you will need two or three volunteers who are well rounded in the business to help create categories.

Break the room for 15 minutes!

THE POST-STORM
CREATING CATEGORIES

I. It is time to start grouping the ideas into two to three categories based on their characteristics.

    a. You and the volunteers have 15-20 minutes to complete the grouping while the larger team is on break.

    b. Examples of groups are: website, app, technology, customer facing, internal improvements, physical product, disruptive service. The groups should be determined by those in the business with the facilitator assisting in creating the groups and discussing.

II. Write each category title at the top of the whiteboard or on each easel note pad.

III. Once you have determined each group, it is time to remove the sticky notes and put them in groups under each group title.

IV. Ask the volunteers if any items can be combined; are there any duplicates? Is each item in the correct group?

V. Organize all the sticky notes into groups and ensure all are stuck on the wall or whiteboard or pads.

VI. Welcome the group back in.

    a. The facilitator is to now share each category with the larger team.

VII. Quickly share each idea that is under each category. *Ask if any are duplicates, can any be combined, are any in the wrong group. (Ask this each time you go over a group.)*

VOTING

I. Now it's time to vote – depending on how many people are in the room, we suggest breaking the group up into three smaller voting bodies. *See Chapter 4 for the formula to determine number of votes.*

II. You will need a lot of room next to the groups and the ideas. If an idea is popular, it will have 20-40 votes and a lot of initials. Make sure to leave a lot of room next to the ideas!

III. Number each category.

IV. Ask each person to count down and give themselves a number. (Yes, the same activity we used in elementary school – 1, 2, 3, 1, 2, 3.)

V. Hand out enough markers so everyone has one.

VI. Remind everyone to vote

VII. Ask each group to stand and go to their corresponding group and vote.

Repeat until all three groups have votes. Break the room for a quick two-minute break!

LET'S PRIORITIZE

I. Facilitator draws the Impact vs. Effort Matrix Graph on the whiteboard.

    a. Impact on Y Axis – Low, Medium, High – 1-10

    b. Effort on X Axis – Easy, Moderate, Difficult – 1-10

    c. Select the first winning idea and the group has open discussion on where it falls on the scale.

    d. Select second, third, fourth, and so on.

    e. Discussion should be "is this easier or harder than that" and some ideas may move locations even after discussion has finished.

II. Be sure everyone is comfortable with where the ideas fall on the scale.

III. The Goal Zone: Medium to High Impact, Easy to Moderate Effort. This is your goal zone; you may want to implement ideas that are in this zone this quarter or this year.

THAT'S A WRAP

I. Facilitator's work is done – count the total ideas.

II. Congratulate the group on coming up with all the impactful ideas; wish those responsible for executing on the winners best of luck, and encourage leadership to schedule a review meeting ASAP to discuss implementation of the winners.

    a. Encourage a future roadmap to review all the ideas.

III. Facilitator takes photos of the idea wall for documentation and sends the total list to the leadership team.

IV. Ask for feedback from entire team. How was it? Surprises? Disappointments?

V. Final words from leadership.

VI. Rate the meeting.

VII. Adjourn.

APPENDIX:
Final Tips for Facilitators

- Review your space ahead of time, typically a day before or hours before so you can get comfortable and get set up.

- Ask for at least one volunteer per hour. Change it up per hour so everyone gets equal time to participate, and the volunteers are not left out.

- Put the summary agenda on a whiteboard. Make sure to have enough storm kit items.

  o Neon sticky notes.

  o Regular small note pads.

  o Music and music box (facilitator should provide).

  o Optional: games, Nerf balls, paper airplanes, masks, other random fun stuff.

APPENDIX:
Innovation Storm Internal Announcement Memo Sample #1 (intro from outside facilitator)

Good evening team,

My name is Justin Waltz, and I am going to be facilitating our up and coming innovation storm, on *date* starting at *time* at the *location title* on *location street address*. You should have already received a calendar invite, so make sure you are available and ready to go.

Justin, what in the world is an innovation storm??

An innovation storm is a collaborative brainstorming event, intended towards generating quantum ideas in a fun and creative setting. Innovation storms take place in large groups with a facilitator and an agenda. The format of a storm is flexible to the goals identified and the disruptive space that is being attacked.

An innovation storm is a high-energy, entertaining, and collaborative session which involves getting everyone together in the organization. It is a fun-filled team-building event with the expectation of coming up with 10x and 100x ideas to grow your business and bring out the next million-dollar improvement or disruptive technology. The goal for the storm is to come up with a vast amount of opportunities for your organization to disrupt your market and gain new business. These opportunities are either to grow and add to your existing business, to grow your existing customer base, or to completely disrupt your market. Additionally, there may be opportunities to enter into a new market or do something completely unconventional from your current organizational model. Think about the Uberization of the taxi cab industry. Think about putting a man on the moon, self-driving and electric cars. From modern streaming subscription-based music to the personal computer, these disruptive innovations have changed our lives.

Starbucks Frappuccino was originally discovered by a group of baristas testing new products in their own store in Southern California. Now it represents over 50% of Starbucks national sales during the summer months… What an awesome disruptive idea, created by the internal team!

Justin, what does that have to do with Company Name?

The exciting news is we are going to get together on *date* and dive deep into the *Company Name* business model, ask a lot of fun questions, and come up with quantum ideas! My events are fun, loud, energetic, and exciting. I promise we will have fun!

Justin, what is the focus? What is the goal?

I had the privilege of spending time with the *Company Name* leadership team to determine the goals for disruption within the *Company Name* family and business model. We came up with four areas to focus on, and we want your help! Four questions (we call these "problem statements") we want to ask, and address during our innovation storm are:

Problem Statements: *(to be addressed on date and time at our in-person event)*

1. **List problem statement #1 here (that you determined with your leadership team)**

2. **List problem statement #2 here (that you determined with your leadership team)**

Okay got it, so how do I come up with big ideas??

Leverage the absurd to discover the powerful. What does this mean? Do not think about restraints such as time, money, resources, people, space, technology, etc. Do not think about any of these restrictions on your ideas. Leverage unlimited amounts of resources, time, money, people, or technology. Think of all of those things as unlimited, and come up with your biggest and best ideas for your business model.

What do we do with our ideas?

If you have a bedside table, write them down on a pad before you go to bed. Take notes in your phone; if you are driving and a great idea comes to mind, pull over and record it in your phone. We all come up with ideas in bed, driving, while taking a shower, and everywhere in between… write them down and bring them to our innovation storm on *date*!

Join our intro call…

I am super excited to work with all of you through this entire creative process. We will have a lot of fun, we will ask hard questions, we will dive deep into the existing business model, and we will challenge all assumptions. This is a creative process with a specific agenda, specific questions to ask each other, and an opportunity for everyone in the organization to speak up. We want to hear from everyone!

I will be holding a 30-minute webinar on *day, date and time* to review the innovation storm agenda with all of you as well as introduce myself, introduce the big questions we are going to ask, and discuss in more detail what the entire day will be like with each other. I also will open the line for any Q&A at the end of the call. I will send out a calendar invite as well! I look forward to meeting all of you soon.

Innovation Storm Internal Announcement Memo Sample #2

Good afternoon, team,

It is with much joy and excitement that we announce that we will be holding a special all-hands meeting on _____, starting at 10 a.m. The purpose of the meeting will be to hold an "Innovation Storm." An innovation storm is a high-energy, goofy, and fun but productive, facilitated meeting where we all will get into a room together and share big ideas to propel our business to new heights and explore ways to disrupt our market. Our goal is always to improve the support of our franchisees, as well as to innovate our products and services we offer to consumers, and what better way to explore new ways of doing so than by hearing from you?

The meeting will be a long one, but we will have fun. Plan on meeting from around 10 a.m. to 3 p.m. as we go down a creative path to explore our business and see where we can go in the future. There is a process and an agenda you will be hearing more about in the coming weeks, and we will hold a conference call to get everyone ready for the meeting.

I look forward to spending this day together, and I know we will come out of the meeting with some great ideas to implement. You will be receiving a calendar invite for the meeting shortly, as well as an invite to the innovation storm pre-call, which will take place a couple of weeks before the meeting.

Have a great day,

BONUS:
Exponentially Grow Your Work & Your Business with a Virtual Team

With the right VA team (Virtual Administrators) you WILL get tons of work done, drastically improve your design and quality of your output, raise your prices, and scale quicker than ever... all while managing a remote workforce of virtual administrators.

The world of virtual administrators and freelance contractors is a competitive, crowded space. However, with the right strategy, some time and patience, and a little bit of luck, you will build a team that will elevate your organization and raise the stakes for you and your work.

Without a strategy and a bit of understanding how to have success with VAs and freelancers, it can be very frustrating working with a remote team, so let's get right to it.

LET'S START WITH THE WHY

Why use freelancers and virtual administrators? First off, there are millions out there performing tasks for as little as $5 that may take you or your team hours or days, and you can save time, which saves money.

Aside from small tasks, there are highly skilled virtual freelancers who you may need for part-time work or project work. Again, having these highly skilled workers available to you will allow you to utilize their skillset without the cost of a full-time employee. This is great for project work, weekly, or monthly tasks/reporting, etc. that only requires a few hours or a few days per month. Freelance help could also be used for a short-term project that you define clearly, and when it is over, you no longer need that skillset anymore.

Lastly, for the WHY: It is so critically important, more than ever, to double down on your strengths and outsource the rest. Dump the workload that is bogging you down every day, and focus on the top 10-20% of what you are great at! Freelancers do exactly that. Break down your day, your week, and your month by tasks you absolutely despise doing. And guess what? That will be the first thing you outsource to a freelancer to learn and test how to properly utilize a freelance team.

Try it with monthly expense reporting, pulling data and organizing the data for your monthly all–staff meeting, booking travel and hotel rooms, designing your company newsletter, building an exquisite PowerPoint presentation, or writing and posting blogs about industry data on your social media site or your company's site. There are thousands of tasks and projects freelancers can help you with. So, the first step is write down the three to five things you absolutely despise doing, or just flat out are terrible at accomplishing. And let's work to freelance those first.

As a tip before getting started and when brainstorming the tasks that you will offload, I recommend you browse tasks and categories of freelance workers and virtual administrators on Upwork.com and Fiverr.com—by browsing, you will see the wide array of who is available and what their skillset is. You can read reviews about graphic designers, branding and marketing experts, data analytics experts and data visualizers, lawyers, writers, editors, sales assistants, and administrative assistants. Browse those two sites to learn more about what they can do.

The Fiverr.com app is great and easy to use. I recommend you download this for simple and quick tasks you need to be completed at your fingertips.

HOW TO GET STARTED:

First, let's start by signing up for accounts with Upwork.com and Fiverr.com and downloading the Fiverr app. The Upwork app is not quite as useful, so I only access Upwork via desktop browser. Complete your profile and upload a professional photo. You may decide to add a company logo. Then let's begin by posting a job – by getting a job posted, you have selected a specific task that you want completed and are now going to put it out there for Upwork contractors to apply to be the one you choose to complete the task monthly.

LET'S POST A TASK

For this example, let's start with this task: "Monthly expense categorization help via excel spreadsheet." (This will be the title of your job.)

For the description, it's best to write a detailed description including a detailed breakdown of what you want completed and how you will get it completed. This is important because you will leave the site for a little while, and when you come back to select your freelancer, if you've already described exactly how you want the job done, then you'll have very little training to do when it's completed.

Here is an example of a description for this task:

We are in search of a virtual administrator to complete the CEO's monthly credit card statement reconciliation report. Approximately 350 charges with many reoccurring charges for easy categorization.

The CEO will provide the spreadsheet template, the categories, account numbers, and each month's credit card statement.

The contractor will receive the statement each month, and we expect the reconciliation report to be completed within three days of receiving the report.

Your first step will be to categorize the reoccurring charges by matching the previous month's charges to any repeated charges.

Your second step will be to Google any unfamiliar charges to determine what the service is (i.e., airline, hotel, restaurant, paid advertising).

Your third step will be to hold a short conference call with the CEO to ask any questions you may have regarding charges and what they are. The CEO will be able to answer most of these quickly.

Once completed, the spreadsheet will be emailed to our accounting department directly from you.

Now that you have written a detailed description including the step-by-step process you will use, the contractors will see that you have clearly defined the task, your posting will be more attractive, and you will have more contractors to choose from. Also, by displaying clear instructions, you have exemplified the ability to communicate and train the contractor easily, thus making you a good client to work for.

SET THE BUDGET

This is where you can use your own discretion—since you are asking for a conference call to clarify any charges, you want a speaker of your native language. If that's English, you may want a freelancer in the US, and if so, you'll pay more money. You can still use an offshore freelancer with English-speaking ability, but communication may be a challenge. You can overcome this by reading the contractor reviews and ratings.

For US workers, you want to set a budget of $7-$10/hour, but this project shouldn't take too long. Maybe one to two hours max.

For offshore workers who may have just as great communication skills, you can pay $4-6/hour.

For skilled work, you will be able to determine costs and average hourly rates based on who is the most active and who has the best reviews. A job posting and project posting is negotiable; you can ask the contractor to name their rate when they apply for the project or task, or you can set a rate you are looking for. I recommend selecting "intermediate" when the website asks for a specific skill range, and going with the rate the website recommends. Then allow contractors to apply for the task or project, and they will propose rates. The proposed rate is negotiable, so you can always ask for a lower rate.

Once you have posted the job, set a detailed description with how the task will be completed and discuss any training or supporting documents. (Tip: if you have a template or examples of the work that has already been completed in the past, you can attach it to the job posting for the contractor to view.) Then you want to set the posting and give it at least 8-12 hours to accept bids.

SELECTING A CONTRACTOR:

Now that you have your job posted, you can begin reviewing your proposals. You can do so as soon as they start coming in, but I recommend waiting 8-12 hours before you start.

Before reviewing proposals, you can browse existing freelancers by clicking through the browse portion of either websites. By doing this, you can view freelancers who match the key words you are looking for in your search. They will have specific skills like administrative, Excel, or spreadsheets.

When looking at an existing contractor you can read reviews and their ratings on their work. Other folks who have hired them will leave comments and rate their work. This is a best practice we will advise for you later on once you have selected a contractor.

Upwork has great filters in place when searching for contractor. You can filter language preferences, how well they know the language, where they are in the world, number of hours worked, and how recently they have performed work.

For Upwork, because of the sheer volume of contractors on the website, I recommend you filter contractor with at least 100 hours of work, active within the last week, and you can check language preferences to your choosing. If you prefer someone work during business hours, you may want to limit where they are around the globe; however, many contractors who do a lot of work with US-based clients have accommodated their working hours to US-based hours, but not all have done this. So, you will have to determine if this is important to you. Especially with the type of task as posed in the example where you ask for a monthly conference call.

Once you have filtered your search, you will receive search results listing contractors that match your request. From here you can click "Invite to your job," and you can invite them to check out your job posting. From here it is up to them if they are interested in your task and if they are currently accepting new clients. Not all contractors will be interested and some are booked full, so it's okay if they decline your request.

Once you have searched and invited people to your job (and you have waited 8-12 hours for people to respond to your posting), it's time to review your candidates.

When reviewing candidates, you will look for number of total hours worked, rating and reviews from clients, examples of the work they have completed, hourly rates for their past projects, hourly rate proposed for this job, and where they are in the world.

Also, you can see things such as testing they have completed to demonstrate their skills, awards they have won for doing a great job (some contractors are in the top 20% of their field or for a specific skill—this is a great thing), and their language abilities.

All of the above are things to consider when choosing your contractor.

For this specific task, I would say an interview is NOT needed;

but an email or chat exchange, or Skype call will be needed to get them started.

If you choose a contractor who is well reviewed and has a good track record, you will have a 90% chance of success, and you'll be on your way to getting tasks done quickly and efficiently… a few hours of work on the front end (posting, training, documenting the steps, and allowing for any questions), and you will soon no longer have to do this task again!

I've hired my contractor—now what?!

Now that you have found the perfect contractor (and let me be clear, you will learn a lot in your selection process, and they all will not turn out great, but it's okay—it may be a trial and error process), you are ready to get started.

LET'S TALK TOOLS

Google Drive & Google Docs – Use this for sharing files, saving documents, and maintaining a weekly status document where your contractor can update their progress, list any questions they have for you, and list the progress of their work. This is a great tool if a contractor is working on multiple projects or tasks. Also on Google Drive, you can create a Google sheet where you share passwords and logins for any specific sites your contractor will need access to. If you do not want them to have your access or your permission levels with certain sites or programs, create a separate login for the administrator and allow them to log in under their own name.

Slack – This is a great collaboration tool for messaging, posting documents, and allowing your contractor to quickly respond to or post questions for you to answer. With Slack you may not need to jump on that Skype call if your contractor can post questions for you to answer quickly.

Zoom Meeting Software – I use Zoom all the time! For hosting meetings BUT also for recording short videos (or long ones). The best way to train a contractor is to have you (or someone on your team who does the task you want completed well) do it first on a computer screen, record it via Zoom, and then save it, upload it to Google drive, and share it. Zoom allows you to host a meeting with yourself, record it, share your screen, speak into your laptop, and record exactly what you are doing and saying. This is HUGE for showing a contractor exactly how you want something done, how to pull data, how to access certain documents, or how to use a proprietary program in an organization.

Tip: if you record your training videos, you never have to train more than once. If you want to hire a new contractor, you already are set up. Same posting, description, documents, and training videos. It gets easier once it's recorded and documented.

Skype – This is great for chatting and also for video calls—most of your contractors will not have a traditional phone line (they cut costs this way), so if you do need to talk to them, plan on doing it by Skype or a Zoom meeting.

Checklist app like ToDoist or Evernote – If you want to create checklists or add tasks to a list for an administrator that's virtual, and allow that person to check off the task once it's been completed (or you can build a training checklist and check off the list once you have trained the person on that topic), I recommend an app that you both can see the checklist and then you both can update, add, delete, and check off as you are working remotely and on projects together. For that specific area, I use ToDoist.

NOW GET TO WORK

Now that you have posted your job, reviewed candidates, selected your contractor, documented exactly what you want done (be super specific; provide screen shots, videos, and allow for a Q&A session), and shared documents and logins, you are ready to sit back and have successfully offloaded that task.

A few hours of work upfront will save you hundreds of hours for years to come. If you follow the above steps and execute well, you can duplicate tasks and hire many freelancer at the same time, or replace a freelancer as needed.

You are now well on your way to employing a remote workforce. Please make sure to leave valuable feedback for your freelancers once they complete the work. They rely on this for future work, especially if they did a great job for you.

Lastly, remain professional and respect their time and skills. Freelancers will rate you as a client as well, and as you build your history and ratings, you will attract better freelancers as you become a reliable source for freelance work. Respect and reviews are a two-way street, and they benefit both the freelancer and the employer.

PART 2
Peer Performance Groups

*"As iron sharpens iron so one man
sharpens another."*
—*Proverbs 27:17*

*"Courage is the resistance to fear, mastery
of fear, not absence of fear."*
—*Mark Twain*

A note from the author

THE TERM MASTERMIND was first introduced by Napoleon Hill in 1925 when he published his book, *The Laws of Success*. However, these "mastermind" alliance and performance groups go back much further in history than just the 1900s, and we will explore the history of mastermind groups and peer performance groups later in this section.

I am an avid reader, mostly non-fiction, and one of my all-time favorite books is *Start With Why* by Simon Sinek. His TED talks have inspired me to become a better leader and a better communicator, and in turn has helped me to build stronger relationships. In everything I do and everything I communicate, I try to determine the why behind it and then communicate the why behind that topic before diving into anything else. Often when speaking in public, teaching, or coaching, I start with why. So here I am starting this section with why peer performance groups are so important. Later on in this section of the book, I will go deeper into how to discover your why with some tips from Simon Sinek, and I'll recommend another one of Simon's books, *Find Your Why*, which describes a system to help you find your why or help you find the why of your entire organization. I want to say thank you to Simon Sinek for publishing such impactful content and videos which I have passed on to so many.

I wrote this section of this book when the concept of mastermind groups or peer performance groups had been proven in multiple franchise systems and in organizations that I had become a part of or had colleagues with whom adopted this concept and the impact it had on the individuals who participated in the groups. The concept of mastermind groups, or peer performance groups, had been a part of my career from almost the first day I hit the real world and got my first "real job."

From the early stages of my career, I was holding networking meetings, best practices meetings, panel of the pros meetings, and even driving up and down Interstate 95 on the east coast of the United States to meet with other business owners in the same industry as myself to learn from them. I formed groups and held conference calls to learn from others who were doing the same job much better than me. And I learned that even after getting experts in a room together, they still could learn from each other as well.

In conference calls, in-person meetings, and events, I became a natural organizer. I was taking copious amounts of notes. I sat in the front of the room and asked questions. I would keep time for people running meetings, and I would even keep parking lots if we went off on tangents and needed to get back on track. Sooner or later people started asking me to facilitate planning meetings, strategic meetings, and mastermind meetings or peer performance groups. At times I would be invited to be part of certain groups that were already formed.

Finally, my career hit a pivotal moment when I was presented with two opportunities. First, I was asked to plan, MC, and host a 250-person annual conference for which I had no idea what I was doing. Second, I was asked to create a new conference, which focused on front-line staff and management staff for franchise owners to attend. All of this in one year.

Over the course of the next year, not only did my team and I put on one of the most successful and impactful annual conventions our organization had ever held (based on feedback surveys and scores), but we also executed on a brand-new conference that saw record attendance and adoption for anything the organization has ever rolled out.

At this point... I now know my why. My why was, and is, to create environments that inspire people to grow, build, connect, and strive to achieve extraordinary results. My mission: To multiply human performance. I knew what I needed to set out to do for the rest of my life. The first step is sharing these tools with you. *I encourage you, at some point, to work on discovering your personal why as well as your organization's why. Once you know your why, navigating the day-to-day drama of life becomes much easier.*

Over the course of a 15-year career in creating mastermind groups, organizing panel of the pros meetings, and facilitating strategic meetings, I became aware of a sixth sense that I created in the room each time I facilitated a meeting. This sixth sense is a sense of energy and dynamic understanding between parties that each person is going to be held accountable, and that together, the group will drive each other to achieve more. Together, performance groups create a team of individuals around each other that are dedicated to each other's success, dreams, visions, and goals. That is how I am able to create extraordinary results through peer performance groups, and I am going to share that with you in this section.

In Part One of this book, you learned how to disrupt your organization with a one-day innovation storm and how to hold the innovation storm flawlessly. With the description, the tools, the agenda, and the kit, by now you should have planned and possibly already executed your one-day innovation storm and are putting action to ideas right away. I am excited for you!

Part Two of this book is about starting and building peer performance groups within your organization for the benefit of you—the reader—and for the accountability and growth of every individual who is willing to participate. As you will learn in this part, peer performance groups are as old as history itself. We know from historians as well as from reading modern era stories that successful business owners, athletes, performers, and musicians did not achieve success alone. In this section of the book, I am going to describe exactly what a peer performance group is, how to form and facilitate a peer performance group, and how to set the stage and mindsets for everyone in the group to have a successful board of personal and professional advisors to guide them, push them further than they knew they could go, and hold each member accountable.

In two parts, this book is about disrupting from within, finding quantum changes within your business, and then holding everyone around you accountable to drive the organization further. By implementing both systems, you not only impact major change, but drive accountability.

I truly believe everyone who sets a big goal and sets out to achieve something deserves a team of individuals holding them to a higher standard, holding them accountable, pushing them to do more, and helping them along the way when they hit obstacles. Anyone who has a dream and a vision deserves a team of people helping them achieve that dream. The groups we create for each other build feedback loops that push people further than they ever dreamed. Everyone deserves to receive feedback from people who care about their success, and everyone deserves the feedback to be direct and in a manner that is built upon information that is shared in a structured setting. A strong peer performance group is not about lecture and facilitation—it's about really pushing each other to succeed and providing feedback every time a meeting comes together. For that, a peer performance group is one of the most powerful systems of accountability there is. For that, each person with a dream and a goal deserves a peer performance group.

Please go out there and create peer performance groups to help yourself grow, and more importantly, help those around you who you know have talent and drive to achieve more. It takes courage and vulnerability to go out and create a world-class team of experts dedicated to your success, but when you do, you'll achieve greater results than you could have ever imagined.

Tony Robbins, the world's top life and strategic coach, often says, "Change your story, change your life," and he says that the three S's of success are state, story, and strategy. A peer performance group will improve your mental state, and help balance your stresses and anxieties by having a sounding board of listeners. You will be able to share your issues and anxieties while receiving feedback on the stories you are telling yourself. An effective peer performance group will be able to tell you if they hear a negative story you are telling yourself. Sometimes it takes a sharp listener to point out negative language we are telling ourselves, and having a group of colleagues listening to you will help point out any excuses or stories you may be telling yourself that could be holding you back. Lastly, Tony mention's strategy as the final step. The truth is that there is plenty of strategy available to all of us. We can visit other organizations, go to conferences, take courses, listen to podcasts, watch YouTube videos, or talk to colleagues.

A true peer performance group will provide feedback on any strategy you are considering, possibly may have already executed on a strategy you are considering, and will be able to provide insights as well. A peer performance group will not only be able to give you feedback on the strategy you are considering, but hold you accountable for tracking your progress and ask for updates along the way. True accountability for all facets of your business or organization, including new strategies you plan to implement.

By now, you should be excited to implement the program outlined in this book. You understand the why, you have a summary definition of what a peer performance group is, you can see how passionate I am about these groups, and you understand what you will benefit from this.

I ask our readers to go out and set aggressive goals. Set and review those goals daily, weekly, monthly, and quarterly. Share your goals with your friends and family, social media, and your peer performance group. I also ask you enroll individuals into this program, aggressively and boldly. You should host meetings or presentations on how you plan to roll this out in your organization. Let your friends and family know that you are seeking a personal and professional board of advisors in the form of a peer performance group. I want you to enroll your closest friends, colleagues, and family, and teach them about this program and the journey you are going to begin. A peer performance group will impact change in your entire life, but first you must get passionate about your success and the success of those around you. By enrolling and letting people know your goals in this journey of forming a peer performance group, your journey will be shared.

Take big action, set big goals, journal and share goals with everyone around you, and enroll others in this program with passion and excitement. Now go get started!

If you enjoy this book and either or both tools, the best acclaim you can give us is to join our private Facebook group, "Disrupt From Within," and post photos and pictures of your innovation storm or peer performance groups. Secondly, the ultimate compliment is if you feel this book is packed with value and you wish to recommend this book to friends, colleagues, and family—I will be very grateful.

Lastly, should you or your organization need assistance in implementing peer performance groups in your organization or franchise system, or seek training or facilitation, we offer professional training and facilitation programs for organizations. Please email JW@JustinWaltz.com for more information.

Justin Waltz

*"An airplane taking off from a runway
requires a tremendous amount of energy and
fuel to build speed and momentum to lift
off the ground, but once off the ground and
flying, tweaks and strategic changes are made
to ensure a smooth and successful flight.
The same can be said for starting a business."*
—Omar Soliman

CHAPTER 1:
Who needs a group?

A PEER PERFORMANCE GROUP is a group of like-minded individuals and professionals who share similar interests to grow and develop themselves and their organizations. They do this by committing to building long-term relationships with accountability partners around them in the form of face-to-face meetings which entail sharing best practices, data, feelings, and working together to set goals and grow both themselves, their leadership skills, and the organizations they have founded or are a part of. Peer performance group members practice confidentiality and agree not to compete against each other. They also hold each other accountable by setting goals and reporting back to each other the status of those goals. A peer performance group is a long-term commitment in which group members agree to push each other, grow together, provide candid feedback with each other, and develop a long-term board of personal and professional advisors for one another. A peer performance group is a life-changing step towards success, and it will multiply your performance as an individual, as well as multiply the performance of your organization.

Based on my stories and descriptions above, you can see that a peer performance group in a small business setting (or a medium or large business) will help tremendously. However, peer performance groups even exist in the form of new mommy groups in hospitals, non-profit organizations sharing information, and teams within or external to any organization. If you are surrounded by individuals within one organization (your workplace, your non-profit organization, your school), then you are getting advice that is siloed and inside a vacuum, based on that organizational culture, goals, or the history you have with the individuals within that organization. By seeking outside advice from others who see things differently, or without history or knowledge from within your organization, you will be able to gain insights on an opportunity or issue you may not have gotten from within the organization. For that reason, it is important to have a diverse group of individuals acting as your personal and professional board of advisors, providing you feedback from their points of view. I encourage anyone who wants to grow any organization to form a peer performance group with individuals who can bring expertise and accountability to each other... From little league commissioners to church leaders, non-profit administrators, new moms, business elites, athletes, artists, musicians, personal trainers, therapists, landscapers, or museum curators. A peer performance group can elevate any group looking to improve in any area.

By taking a 30,000-foot view of your business or organization, you are getting out of the day-to-day minutia of your role and taking a hard look at the systems, plans, goals, and strategies of your organization, which allows you to impact change and make actionable deviations in strategy and execution when you get back to the day-to-day operations of your organization.

This book will describe specific systems and methods to execute on performance groups in a business setting which will be very applicable to some of the examples I mentioned above.

For franchise systems, businesses, non-profits, and small business owners, the following peer performance group systems should be followed as closely as possible.

Note: Peer performance groups do not need to be local. We

prefer they are not local because the ability to travel and get away from your business, department, or organization allows you to get out of your element and disconnect for a couple of days. This system allows you to take a high-level view of your business or organization.

For a complete list of who a peer performance group applies to, please see the appendix for more details.

"Analyze the record of any man who has accumulated a great fortune, and many of those who have accumulated modest fortunes, and you will find that they have either consciously, or unconsciously employed the 'Master Mind' principle."
—Napoleon Hill, Author of Think and Grow Rich

VALIDATION: THE UNSUNG HERO OF SUCCESS

Validation is one of the unsung heroes of success and often one of the most forgotten or most unspoken benefits of a peer performance group. Validation comes in the form of our peers helping us achieve fulfillment and gratitude by reminding us of the reasons we got started in the first place, reminding us that we have achieved a level of success we may have become blind to, and reminding us to be grateful for the path we have carved already and the achievements we have accomplished. When we are up against deadlines or grinding day in and day out, it can be tough to step away and just appreciate what we have. A peer performance group provides the opportunity to do just that. Validation is confirmation that we are doing the right things and that what we are trying to accomplish is going to be hard and the struggle is part of the process. Validation also comes in the form of comparing data to show us that we are succeeding with a new product launch or a new marketing program, or that the business is profitable. There is nothing more demeaning than comparing your business to something or someone with no context or nothing to compare to. A peer performance group allows you to compare and often validates that what you are doing is what you should be doing.

Whether it be in the form of data and comparing information, adding gratitude to your life, fulfillment through helping others, or just realizing that the struggles you are going through and the issues you are facing are normal for the growth you are experiencing, a peer performance group can provide much needed validation which will be the fuel that keeps you driving forward toward your vision and goals.

CHAPTER 2:
Peer Performance Groups:
A history lesson

PEER PERFORMANCE GROUPS, mastermind groups, growth groups, momentum groups, and flight groups are just a few of the numerous names we have seen for these types of teams. In this chapter, we will explore the history of peer performance groups to embrace these concepts in even more detail.

KING ARTHUR & THE KNIGHTS

One could say one of the first mastermind groups to be mentioned in history is King Arthur and the Knights of the Roundtable. King Arthur, Lancelot, and the roundtable have been written about in history books as both history and fable. The concept of the round-table and the concept of open and honest feedback through the roundtable is something that still holds true in modern era business and organizations. A mastermind or peer performance group meeting often happens in a roundtable format, and history shows us that King Arthur may have been the one to make the roundtable famous.

FRANKLIN D. ROOSEVELT

In politics and government, in today's era, advisors and experts are very common. One of the first mastermind groups or board of advisors in politics was a group of academic elites brought in to advise Franklin Roosevelt during his presidential term—this group helped him to develop critical laws still in place today and played a major role in the enactment of laws enacted in the early 1900s. During his two-term presidency, the government instituted a series of experimental projects and programs, known collectively as the New Deal, for which many believe this advisory panel played a huge role in.

CARNEGIE AND THE STEEL TITANS OF AMERICA

Andrew Carnegie is known as the American steel industry titan. Many believe without the work of Andrew Carnegie, what we know as the skyscraper today would not exist. It is known that Andrew Carnegie did not know the most about steel or how to produce steel, but he knew people, and he knew how to interact and surround himself with the best people in the industry. Napoleon Hill wrote in his book, *Think and Grow Rich,* about Andrew Carnegie and his ability to surround himself with the best people. Long before the term "mastermind" was even invented, Mr. Carnegie had a close group of advisors pushing him and his team to succeed. Hill writes of the energy created by a "sixth sense" when minds come together, and Mr. Carnegie took full advantage of this. It is safe to say that the American industrial revolution and the titans that led the movement, did so with the power of peer performance groups.

Napoleon Hill, in his book, Think and
Grow Rich, *defines a mastermind as
"coordination of knowledge and effort, in
spirit of harmony, between two or more
people, for the attainment of a definite
purpose."*

THE JUNTO

The Junto, one of the best names of a mastermind group so far as written in history, was comprised of Benjamin Franklin, the founder. Franklin wanted to establish himself with a group of working-class tradesmen and artisans. The group originally held 12 members, and Franklin referred to the group as a "mutual improvement society." The club, founded in 1727, met every Friday evening, and lasted 38 years! It was also known as the Leather Apron Club. If you are interested in this specific meeting, Benjamin Franklin published a list of questions to guide discussions at meetings. A list of these questions is provided in the appendix at the end of this book.

THE VAGABONDS

The Vagabonds are one of the most iconic business mastermind groups to ever be discussed in history. Starting in 1916, Thomas Edison, Henry Ford, Harvey Firestone, and Warren G. Harding would go camping in the wilderness together to share stories, discuss strategy, and work together to prioritize and advise each other on each of the men's companies. What a group! What a brain trust! We are talking about the Ford Model T production discussions, the modern era tire, and countless ideas and iconic business decisions we know today, being discussed and advised upon in this group. What an astounding group.

THE FOUR HORSEMEN

An article published by the *New York Times*, shares that Lebron James has an entourage, which I know doubles as a peer performance group and support group of his closest friends. Lebron James is known as one of the greatest athletes of all times. Lebron is also known as one of the biggest brands in sports marketing and business. At the age of 19, and as his career progressed, Lebron hired three close friends who he had known since childhood. His childhood friends, who he trusted, became his agent, brand ambassador, and CEO of his brand. The four of them became known as The Four Horsemen, and they went on to emboss a symbol of a knight onto their sneakers.

FACEBOOK GROUPS OR MEETUP.COM

Our favorite websites to find peer performance groups or start a peer performance group are Meetup.com and Facebook Groups.

The groups just discussed represent powerful mastermind groups from historical record to modern era. As mentioned, those who have led businesses, governments, or even economic or technological revolutions, did not do it alone. Peer performance groups or mastermind groups have shown to be a tremendous (and even a bit of a secret) tool of the ultra-successful. You deserve a group of supporters pushing you to achieve greatness and helping you keep the momentum. Even more importantly, as we see from the previous discussion, who you select to be a part of your mastermind group can have a major impact on the level of achievement within the group, so choose wisely. In the following chapter, we will discuss how to structure a mastermind group and options for the structure. Structure is extremely important in your mastermind group, because the top two reasons a mastermind group will fail is lack of structure and lack of facilitation. Let's dive into structure!

CHAPTER 3:
An ounce of prevention is worth more than a pound of cure

WHY DO PEER PERFORMANCE GROUPS FAIL?

1. Lack of structure

2. Lack of facilitation

3. Too frequent of meetings or dilution of the meetings

4. Lack of commitment

LACK OF STRUCTURE

Your peer performance group should have a set agenda which allows members to understand the flow and the dynamic of each meeting. The structure should include a general breakdown of time allotted for each section of the meeting. Along with structure, rules and mindsets are a good idea to review before each meeting, and we are going to recommend a conference call with meeting attendees before each meeting happens to review the meeting rules, mindsets, structure, and to discuss logistics of the upcoming meeting. We will also discuss how to include a parking lot. A parking lot is an area or whiteboard we use to write in discussion topics when a meeting goes off on a tangent. Often, those tangents are impactful discussions that will require more time than the current agenda item has allotted. We will put the topic and specific points on the parking lot, and then we will leave time in the meeting, usually designated on the agenda as "parking lot," to discuss the items. These tangents are important, and we do want to get to them, but a good facilitator will know when to announce to the group that we need to parking lot the items and get back on track.

A well-planned agenda and structure, along with defined mindsets and rules, combined with a pre-arrival conference call will allow for a great meeting each time, and will set the expectation of each member before each meeting. This will ensure consistency throughout the life of the peer performance group. We even leave room for housekeeping items in the agenda, which can include discussing the structure of the meeting—this allows for members to discuss whether they want to make changes to the structure of the group or the agenda of each meeting.

LACK OF A STRONG FACILITATOR OR FACILITATION AT ALL

A strong facilitator, who keeps the meeting on point and on agenda, is critical to the success of any meeting, let alone a successful peer performance group. All peer performance groups should have a facilitator who is responsible for keeping the meeting on pace. A strong facilitator carries empathy for all meeting attendees. This means the facilitator has the best interest of all meeting attendees at heart and is not one that is going to rule the meeting. No facilitator should speak the most at the meeting. The facilitator role can rotate among members for peer performance groups that are outside of professional environments. For professional peer performance groups, small business groups, and non-profits, it is advised that an outside member of the group be brought in to facilitate the meetings. Facilitators are responsible for ensuring the meeting space is well suited, the meetings are entertaining and comfortable, and logistics are set and coordinated. This book will give plenty of advice for future facilitators as we discuss structure and agendas in the next few chapters. For more information on professional facilitation of peer performance groups or facilitation training, email JW@JustinWaltz.com to learn about our available services.

TOO FREQUENT OF MEETINGS OR DILUTION OF MEETINGS

Peer performance groups are meant to be your personal and professional board of advisors, with members who are going to push you and your business to set aggressive goals and hit those goals faster than you would have without your performance group. This means the meetings have to be taken seriously, and members must fully commit to each other.

A common reason peer performance groups fall apart is the dilution of the meeting by way of the members' attitudes, or even the frequency of the meetings. If your members all live in the same town and do not commit to the meetings because they happen every two weeks, or even once a month, and the facilitation is lackluster, then you will not carry momentum from meeting to meeting, and thus, it will fall apart.

With less frequent meetings and further distance between group members, you may find that the meetings are stronger. In writing this book, our vision is of a peer performance group meeting in which members value their time with one another and spend time not only in formal meeting settings, but also with each other individually to get to know each other. One could say that a peer performance group meeting should almost be a retreat, and many successful groups do see them as such. They spend time with their peer groups to unplug, get to know each other, discuss hot topics or opportunities, and dive deeper into their interests and into each other.

We encourage you to create a group that meets less frequently if needed, but have longer meetings when you do get together. It is advised to go offsite, a place where you can concentrate and enjoy your time together.

By choosing committed members, implementing a structure

that everyone agrees to and understands, and carefully considering the frequency of your meetings as well as considering how geography plays a part in the meetings, you can ensure your peer performance groups will avoid the mistakes that will lead to failure.

"I get up every morning determined to both change the world and have one hell of a good time. Sometimes this makes planning my day difficult."
—E.B. White

CHAPTER 4:
The structure –
The business/non-profit peer performance group

IN THE FOLLOWING chapter, we are going to dive into the structure and format of a business or non-profit mastermind group that meets less frequently, with geography not being important at all. This is the most successful format as this format will assume meetings with a frequency of twice a year, three times a year, or, at max, four times a year (quarterly meetings). This type of meeting will last between two and a half to three days, and will assume a retreat style meeting. This meeting is great for small business owners of the same industry/trade, franchisees, franchisors, non-profit administrators, executives of large corporations in the same organization, executives of large corporations in the same industry but not competing, or coaching/athletics organizations not competing against each other. For a full list of who can benefit from a peer performance group, please see the appendix.

THE BIRD'S EYE VIEW

From a bird's eye, high-level summary, this peer performance group will function best with 6-10 members max. We suggest three or four times per year for maximum impact. The schedule and the meetings require a meeting facilitator, either outside the group as an extra member or with the facilitator role rotating among members. It is important to ensure the elected facilitator reads this book each time and understands what makes a great facilitator.

Each year the group meets, it will consist of a setup/welcome email with instructions, a pre-arrival conference call, the collection of prep work, the arrival day, two days of meetings, and then a travel day. In the following chapter, we will review each of these sections in detail to ensure they are executed well. A well-organized peer performance group has expectations set ahead of time, and, thus, all members know what to do and when to do so.

THE KICKOFF CONFERENCE CALL & REVIEW OF MINDSETS

To start your very first peer performance group meeting, you want to ensure an extraordinary kickoff call. If you are the curator of the group and the one who championed the idea in the first place, then you will run the kickoff call. If you are the one who helped select the first few group members (if not all of them), then you may be the lifetime facilitator, or you may choose to bring in outside facilitation. Either way, the kickoff call will be important to set the precedent for the future of the group. Groups may choose to bring in outside facilitation after a meeting or two. It is often found that some group members make great facilitators, while others not so much. For executive peer performance groups, small- to medium-sized peer performance groups, and franchisee or franchisor peer performance groups, it is advised that a facilitator be utilized. Group members can also attend peer performance group facilitator training—resources for both are listed at the end of this book.

Note: Facilitators come in all forms. They can be a colleague in a different department, a business area leader, an executive c-suite leader, a fellow franchisee, or a professional facilitator whom has no connection to the businesses. Selecting a strong facilitator will greatly improve the success rate of the group and make for less stressful, more focused meetings.

"Empathy first, creativity second. These are the two most critical traits of any strong facilitator and meeting planner. You must be able to place yourself in the shoes of the attendees every step of the way."
—Justin Waltz

During the kickoff call and during almost every welcome/pre-arrival call, it is essential that the facilitator (or the curator of the mastermind group if it's the first call), review the four mindsets for creating lifeline relationships. In his book, *Who's Got Your Back: The Breakthrough Program to Build Deep, Trusting Relationships That Create Success and Won't Let You Fail,* Keith Ferrazzi outlines these four critical mindsets.

MINDSET #1: GENEROSITY

In his book, Ferrazzi outlines that it is almost impossible to be negative or be in a victim mindset when we are practicing generosity in our daily lives and also in our peer performance groups. Generosity can come in the form of helping others once we determine how we can serve them, and it can also come in the simplest form of connecting with another person and empathizing or caring for their situation.

Another critically important part of generosity is the ability to accept another person's generosity towards you, the receiver. In his book, Ferrazzi states, "Whether we realize it or not, this willingness to 'give and let give' creates a wonderful give-and-take in a relationship."

MINDSET #2: VULNERABILITY

Vulnerability is one of the biggest character traits important to creating lifelong relationships, and Ferrazzi tells us that it is key. Vulnerability is the courage to show your fears, your struggles, and your inner thoughts, and allow those around you to help. It requires you to admit your weaknesses and share exactly what you are thinking. Vulnerability also requires you be proactive in your approach to building relationships. You do not have to be vulnerable—you must make the choice to practice vulnerability. This means admitting fault and fears, and opening up and presenting these to the group. Your inner circle may not proactively seek to go deeper with you until you reveal what exactly you are struggling with. However, when you do, you invite those around you to help you and share with you. The beauty of vulnerability is that it's contagious in nature. The more vulnerable group members become with one another, the more others will open up. We will practice vulnerability in the meeting ice breakers and morning check-in. This is the perfect time to start practicing vulnerability, and we have shared a list of ice breakers that help with vulnerability in the appendix of this book.

MINDSET #3: CANDOR

Candor is defined by the *Merriam-Webster Dictionary* as unreserved, honest, or sincere expressions. Keith Ferrazzi describes candor as the ability to engage in healthy, caring, and purposeful criticism. We consider candor to be the ability to not hold back and always be providing feedback, in a tactful manner. From our observations of many peer performance groups, executive retreats, quarterly and annual planning meetings, and high performing teams, candor is one of the biggest differences in high performing teams and is a big part of what drives success for every team member.

An important factor when discussing candor with a group is the fact that every group member has been selected to be a part of the group. For that reason, everyone has input that has already been identified as a benefit for each of the other group members. Be it your experience, your background, education, network, or any other reason, your feedback is needed for the betterment of each group member. For that reason, candor is expected out of each member. If you are holding back from delivering feedback to one of your group members, you are practicing a lack of integrity. We believe all feedback is a gift, and, thus, being part of the group deems your feedback valuable and important, and it should be said.

The ability to receive feedback is just as important as the ability to give feedback. Candor requires all members of the group to understand that all feedback is a gift. Receiving negative or challenging feedback can be tough. Maturity and personal and professional growth among group members requires the ability to receive all feedback in a manner that shows appreciation and understanding among the group members who give the feedback.

The skill of giving and receiving feedback and practicing candor in group meetings is one that requires time to develop. The quicker a group can create a trusting environment, where all members feel comfortable sharing open and honest feedback through being candid and vulnerable, will propel the group to achieve success. It is essential for group members and facilitators to discuss the importance of candor, describe what it is, and work on improving candor within the group before, during, and after each meeting.

MINDSET #4: ACCOUNTABILITY

With the previous three mindsets in mind, you can almost guarantee that accountability will be present within your peer performance group. Accountability is the capacity to hold group members responsible for what they say they are going to do and within what time frame they are going to do it. As part of the checkout process in group meetings, we ask members to define what exactly it is they are going to do after the meeting to make an impact on their future. As Ferrazzi explains in his book, the right accountability partner or group is essential to hitting your goals.

Sometimes your friends and family are too close to you to hold you truly accountable, but a strong peer performance group can be a powerful reinforcing mechanism.

We recommend you review the above mindsets at each meeting and during each pre-call with the entire group. For quick reference, we've added them to the appendix.

THE KICKOFF CALL — YOUR VERY FIRST CALL AS A NEW GROUP

In the beginning of the first conference call—the kickoff call—thank and welcome all your group members to the newly formed peer performance group. It is a great idea at the beginning of your call to recommend that each member read this book if you have not already done so. The following agenda below will describe the format and structure to follow on your kickoff call. The kickoff call is the first call your group ever has, so you'll want to follow this agenda and send it to your attendees ahead of time.

For the first call, you want to follow this agenda:

1. Welcome to the group & group reading recommendations (this book)

2. Review the four mindsets and explain each (listed in this chapter and the appendix)

3. Group member introductions

    a. Who you are, where you are from

    b. Professional background

4. Share each member's three-year professional vision and 10-year b-hag (big hairy audacious goals)

5. Share the reason(s) they joined the peer performance group

6. Share an ice breaker (since this is a phone call, we recommend a lighter ice breaker)

CHAPTER 5:
The agenda for the peer performance group meeting

Here is an overview of the agenda for the two-day peer performance group meeting for businesses, non-profits, and franchisees or franchisors. In this chapter, we will describe, in detail, each day and each component of the peer performance group meeting. All supporting material needed for the group meeting, including guides for the pre-work, will be included in the appendix at the end of this book.

Agenda for Peer Performance Group
(Insert clever group name here)
Pre-Arrival Call (two weeks prior to meeting)
Arrival day
Host presentation day
Peer presentation day
Adjourn

THE PRE-ARRIVAL CALL

The pre-arrival call is to engage members of the group for the upcoming mastermind meeting. This call is to go over the following:

- Arrival and departure times, logistics, and who's renting a car, if anyone.

- Review the four mindsets (see appendix).

- Review pre-work requirements.

- Allow the host to welcome the group with any information about dinner plans, activities scheduled, weather and what to wear, and information about the host city.

- Review the location of the meeting, how to get to it or check in, and how members plan to get there.

- Review the agenda, ask if anyone has any special requests for agenda items, and ensure everyone is clear on the agenda for the two-day meeting.

- Review the meeting check-in process and check-out process with S.M.A.R.T. goals. S.M.A.R.T. goals are defined as simple, measurable, attainable, realistic, and timely.

- Discuss extracurricular activities. It is common to have an early arrival day and for the host to arrange and participate in a fun team-building activity. Some activities we've seen that are popular are golf, fishing, hiking, paintball, museum tours, bike rides, and go-cart racing. Hosts are encouraged to be creative when planning team-building events or activities to showcase their city.

Note: At the time this book was published, Airbnb, the online marketplace for short term lodging, is a great place to find large homes to host mastermind meetings. It has also added experiences to book at host cities. Checkout the Airbnb app for planning meeting locations and activities to do with your groups.

Here is a detailed description of each portion of this kickoff call.

ARRIVAL & DEPARTURE TIMES

It is a good idea to gather each person's arrival times with airline and airport information. Some cities have multiple airports, so it is important to know who's arriving at what airport. List on the agenda the arrival and departure times, airport, and cell phone of each member. Members can share a rental car or rideshare cost if they are arriving at the same time. After the pre-arrival call, send out the information to all members as part of the full agenda.

THE FOUR MINDSETS

Review with all members on each pre-arrival call the four mindsets of a successful peer performance group. They can be easily found at the end of this book in the appendix.

THE PRE-WORK REQUIREMENTS

For businesses, franchisors, franchisees, and non-profits, we highly suggest your members submit pre-work prior to attending the meeting. Each member will be required to submit pre-work in a shared folder for members to review prior to the meeting. We will go into detailed suggestions for pre-work in this chapter, but for the pre-arrival call, review all pre-work requirements and ensure all members know exactly what is requested, what the layout and format of each document should be, and how to submit or share the work. It is a good idea to provide examples of each pre-work submission to set proper expectations.

THE HOST WELCOMES THE GROUP

On the pre-arrival call, allow some time for the host to give some welcoming information about the upcoming trip. Discuss where the group will be staying, ideas for dinner each evening, and the potential activities the group could participate in. Or the host can poll the group for which activities they'd like to do. Also, the host should give a weather report for each day and night so the group knows what exactly to wear for the meeting, the evenings, and the activities.

REVIEW THE LOCATION OF THE MEETING

If you are holding a retreat, staying in a home, a resort, or staying in a hotel, review the details of where the place is, what the check-in procedures are, times for check-in and check-out, and allow group members to ask any questions about lodging.

REVIEW THE AGENDA

Briefly run through the agenda for the entire group. This will ensure everyone has read it and knows what to expect for the two days together.

REVIEW THE CHECK-IN AND CHECK-OUT PROCESS FOR THE MEETING

After this section, we will go into detail about the check-in and check-out process. To ensure you set expectations of an on-time start and how exactly the meeting will start, review the check-in questions that you will ask each group member to respond to. Also, ensure to describe to the group at the end of Day 2 the process of setting S.M.A.R.T. goals for each other to report back to the group at the next meeting. We will review S.M.A.R.T. goals and the check-in and check-out process in the next chapter. As a reminder, S.M.A.R.T. goals are defined as simple, measurable, attainable, realistic, and timely.

DISCUSS EXTRACURRICULAR ACTIVITIES

For the final part of the pre-arrival call, discuss any extracurricular activities the facilitator or the host have considered for the group. Take a poll of who wants to do what, or leave it open and ask for suggestions. It is a good idea to arrive early on the first day and participate in a group team-building activity, or stay an extra day after meetings to enjoy some time together. Whatever you decide as a group, make sure it's a group choice and go have some fun together!

ADJOURN

End the call allowing for an open floor for questions and discussion. Enthusiastically let the group know how excited you are to facilitate and see everyone.

DAY 1:
The Arrival

The arrival day is exactly as it sounds. It is the day the group arrives to the city and to the location of the meeting. Your group may decide to take early flights or drive early in the morning to arrive to their destination with time to meet for an extracurricular activity or team-building activity. As part of the pre-arrival call, we discussed setting the expectations for arrival day. Some group members prefer to arrive early to allow themselves time to check in, get settled, complete any additional pre-work, spend time reading the other group members' pre-work, or just to take a break and unplug from their businesses or organizations. It is important to have a relaxing arrival day to allow members to get to know each other and settle in. The arrival day also allows time for any unfortunate travel delays that do sometimes happen when groups travel. Ensure not to schedule anything too firm that may be at risk of a travel delay.

The arrival day dynamic will continue to improve throughout the lifecycle of the group, and your members will get more creative on what to do for arrival day. For the evening of arrival day, ensure to have a kickoff meal together. This is a low-key, relaxing dinner where members can start to get to know each other and understand the challenges they are facing. Over this first dinner, new groups will often discuss each other's family, hobbies, backgrounds, and everything in between.

A peaceful arrival day will ensure a great two days of meetings that follow.

DAY 2:
The Host Presentation

The host presentation day is specific to small, medium, or large business groups, franchisors, franchisees, and non-profit organizations. The host presentation is a full one-day deep dive into the organization or business of the host. This is a special day as it is an opportunity for the host to ask the group members to take a deep dive into their organization, peel back all the layers, and at the end of the day, provide feedback for the host based on their observations and group discussion. The host presentation consists of the following agenda items:

- Check in & ice breaker
- Update on goals from last meeting (facilitator presents S.M.A.R.T. goals from previous meeting - S.M.A.R.T. goals are defined as simple, measurable, attainable, realistic, and timely.)
- The host presentation
- The host data & key performance indicators review
- Optional: team member interviews
- The host request for information presentation
- Group feedback discussion
- Feedback presentation and validation from host
- Adjourn for happy hour

THE CHECK-IN

The check-in sets the stage for the entire meeting. The group should be settled in, seated, note pages ready, morning beverages in hand, and ready to go. The facilitator should welcome the group, thank everyone for being there, recap the prior evening, and ask one more time if everyone is set to get started.

For the check-in, the facilitator must ask everyone to answer, in depth as much as they choose, the following three questions, plus add an ice breaker. (Ice breaker questions are listed at the end of this book in the appendix.)

The four-step check-in questions are as follows: (*Note: These questions are vague for a reason; encourage members to interpret and answer them as they see fit, to emphasize creativity and vulnerability.*)

- How are you feeling?
- What are you leaving behind personally and professionally?
- What are your goals for the week?
- The ice breaker question. (See appendix for ice breaker questions.)

The check-in process is meant to set the stage (after the facilitator reviews the mindsets), for vulnerability and candor for the rest of the meeting. Group members may, and are encouraged to, share as much as they like. Do not rush this process as it is a time for everyone to step into the meeting and lean into each other, building chemistry by sharing what is going on in their personal and professional lives and why they are attending the meeting. You will learn what they are looking for from the group and maybe a specific business issue they wish to tackle for their time together with you.

If you are meeting for a few days, pick an in-depth ice breaker that will provoke thought and vulnerability. The ice breakers we have listed in the appendix are deep and thought provoking. If you feel the group is not ready for a deep dive ice breaker, you can Google "meeting ice breakers" to get easier, light-hearted ice breakers.

As the facilitator, encourage strong check-ins, and make a habit of starting on time, with everyone aware of the check-in process. With time, check-ins become stronger and members reveal more info. *Hint: Make sure to participate in the check-in as the facilitator, and show vulnerability. The other group members will catch on by your example.*

UPDATE ON THE GOALS FROM THE PREVIOUS MEETING

As part of the check-in process, after everyone has completed the round of answers from above and participated in the ice breaker, it is time to share the goals from the previous meeting. These S.M.A.R.T. goals should be projected for everyone to see or printed onto a handout. We suggest going in the same order as the check-in and ask members to update the status of each goal. Everyone should report how it went implementing or executing the change, how the change has impacted the organization, and any supporting facts or follow-up information the group should know.

If a goal has not been completed, as the facilitator, ask the group to work with the member to determine if it is a carry over or if the goal should be eliminated and why. To achieve commitment from the group, we want to ensure accountability is happening during the goal review. If a goal is not achieved, take the time to discuss why, and if it is determined that a goal will be eliminated, discuss why and how to avoid it in the future. The facilitator's commitment to driving accountability through the goal setting and review process will encourage the group to set aggressive and S.M.A.R.T. goals.

THE HOST PRESENTATION

Congratulations, the check-in, and update on previous goals have all been completed, and now the meeting is off and running. It is time for the in-depth host presentation. The host presentation format is long and extremely detailed. For that, we have placed it in the appendix at the end of this book. You will want to share the host presentation format with the host, and allow the host at least four weeks to prepare the presentation.

Note: Break the room for a coffee refill or restroom break prior to starting the host presentation.

The host presentation and agenda for the day consists of the following parts:

- Your personal history
- Your professional history
- Your history with your current organization
- Your organizational structure
- Your organizational chart and description of key personnel
- Personnel compensation and benefits
- Your business/organizational performance
- Your approach to the marketplace and marketing techniques
- Your customer interaction and your sales lifecycle (what business you are in and what business you want to be in, what journey you put your customers through)
- Innovation: what areas of your business need innovation, what you are currently innovating, or what you want help from the group to innovate
- Optimization and Maximization: Capacity and KPI's
- Optional: meeting of key team members
- Presentation of RFIs (Requests for information)
- Feedback loop with peer performance group members
- Feedback delivery
- Validation
- Adjourn

The host presentation is detailed and in-depth. **The appendix contains the details with a step-by-step guide on how to create the host presentation.** Ensure each host gets the guide with enough time to answer the questions, pull the data, and reflect on the challenges and issues to put forth in front of their board of advisors. The presentation guide is meant to walk them through exactly how to come up with content for the presentation; however, it does take time to complete. It is a best practice to encourage each host to spend time in silence and without distraction preparing their presentation. The host will want to allow time for the answers to come to them and allow time for edits where needed as the event gets nearer.

A well-crafted host presentation will provide the host with world-class feedback from the group and a laundry list of actions to take as well as innovative ways to approach their business after the meeting. Think of the host presentation as a major opportunity to deep dive into your business or organization with your peer performance group, dedicated to providing you with new opportunities to improve and grow, for one full day. This is an incredible opportunity a host will not want to take lightly.

Utilize the detailed host presentation in the appendix for each presentation.

THE HOST'S KEY PERFORMANCE INDICATORS & FINANCIAL DATA REVIEW

After the host presentation, the host then goes into sharing data and key performance indicators. Organizations will share data based on what is available to them. It is a good idea to start with basics such as financial statements (profit and loss, balance sheet, and the statement of cash flows) and key performance indicators the group can compare to one another. This can be marketing expenses, ROI on marketing efforts, labor efficiency and labor costs, asset costs, capacity reports, inventory reports, customer saturation metrics, and beyond.

Note: It is important to discuss with your peer performance group which data would be best to see and compare among group members. Data comparison will evolve as the group becomes more in tune with each other's businesses. It is a good idea to discuss comparing data, which data group members would like to see, and in which format— this should be discussed after each meeting during the parking lot or housekeeping sessions and before the group adjourns.

OPTIONAL TEAM MEMBER INTERVIEWS: FOR LEADERS WHO HAVE DIRECT REPORTS IN LEADERSHIP POSITIONS

The team member interview portion of the host presentation day can be challenging, but when prepared correctly, expectations set with the team members, and the actual interview executed well, it can be one of the most powerful portions of the day and improve the quality of the feedback delivered to the host at the end of the day.

The team member interview is for any host that is in a leadership position and has other leaders directly reporting to them.

Another example is the founder of a business or organization who will have an executive suite of leadership, middle managers, sales staff or office staff directly reporting to the owner. If the owner is the host for the peer performance group, then an interview with one or more of these direct reports can prove extremely valuable to learn more about the leadership style of the host, strengths and weaknesses of the host, and areas for improvement.

The first step for setting up the interview process with team members of the host is to have the host prepare the leadership team member for the interview process. It is a good idea to either send them information about the peer performance group via email or have a face-to-face meeting about the interview. The introduction can go something like this:

Good morning,

I have enrolled in a peer performance group with individuals from our industry around the country who are dedicated to help each other grow personally and professionally, and improve each other's businesses. A peer performance group is a personal and professional board of advisors.

The exciting news is that I am hosting a peer performance group meeting in our city next week, and the group would love to meet some of our leaders to better understand our business and my leadership style. I would love if you would spend an hour with the group next week to allow them to ask you a few questions and discuss the organization and my leadership abilities. I will not be in the room, and the group will ask for your candidness in order to ensure I am getting the best feedback. This is a great opportunity for you to point out areas I can improve and big opportunities you see within our organization. They may ask to meet with other team members, but for today, I would love to recommend they meet with you.

Come see me or give me a call when you get this information—I would like to discuss the format with you, give you an under-standing of who the group members are and their background, and answer any questions you may have.

Don't worry, the group is friendly and extremely knowledgeable. They have only the best intentions to help our organization grow and help me grow as a leader. Please let me know if you have any questions.

Best,

Your name

The leadership team member interview is a great way to dive into the business or organization as well as get an understanding of the perception of the host from the team members. It will allow the peer performance group to understand how the host can become a better leader. Here is a list of the top questions to ask leadership team members who report directly to the owner.

- Please introduce yourself and give us your professional background prior to joining this organization, your history within this organization, and your current role.

- What do you do on a day-to-day basis? What do you do in your current role?

- How often do you interact with *your host?* How do you receive formal feedback about the performance of the organization as well as your performance in your role?

- What are the biggest strengths of *your host* as a leader of this organization?

- What are the weaknesses of *your host* as a leader of this organization?

- What are the biggest current threats and challenges to this organization?

- What is the one-year strategic plan and the three-year vision of this organization? Has *your host* clearly defined these?

- What is at least one thing *your host* should stop doing related to leading and growing this organization to achieve the one-year strategic plan and three-year vision?

- What is at least one thing *your host* should start doing related to leading and growing this organization to achieve the one-year strategic plan and three-year vision?

- What is at least one thing *your host* should keep doing related to leading and growing this organization to achieve the one-year strategic plan and three-year vision?

- As *your host's* professional and personal board of advisors, where would you like to see this group focus our attention in working with *your host*? What is the best use of our time?

- Do you feel you spend a majority of your time fixing problems or creating systems and growing the organization?

- What questions do you have for this peer performance group, or are there any other facts or opportunities we should know about as a group to improve our advisory responsibilities to *your host*?

The host leadership team interview process can be extremely eye opening for the peer performance group. The above questions can provide insights about the host and the host's organization which will evolve into valuable feedback for the host. By using the above questions, you will learn more about the host's leadership style, the perception of the individuals who report to the host, and the biggest opportunities for the host and the organization to improve.

One person should lead the interview process, but the group members may chime in throughout and ask their own questions. All members should be taking notes throughout the meeting with the leadership team members and listening for areas of opportunity and feedback to be delivered to the host.

When executed properly, the team member interview process can open opportunities for the organization and provide valuable feedback to the host. Next, we will explore how feedback is organized and delivered to the host.

---

*"Every now and then you should try to do the impossible, because not only do you discover why it's impossible, but it allows you to stretch the imagination.
You have to blur the edge between the impossible and the possible."*
—*Walter Isaacson*

THE HOST'S PRESENTATION OF RFIS (REQUESTS FOR INFORMATION)

The request for information is the part of the day where the host gets to direct the peer performance group to areas of their business and life they'd like help with. The request for information is an opportunity to really dive into issues and opportunities with the entire group. This is where the concept of a personal and professional board of advisors really takes shape. During the presentation, the group is asking questions, taking notes, discovering opportunities for the host and providing feedback.

The request for information is a combination of organic facts and feelings with data and additional information added to paint the best picture for the group. The request for information can be an opportunity, a personnel change or elimination, a position or role addition, a big assumption based on data, a hunch that needs work, or even an outcry for help in a certain area.

As part of the host presentation, a host can (and we encourage the host to) deliver multiple requests to the group.

The request for information should be executed in this order:

- State the opportunity, challenge, hunch, position or person to be discussed, issue, or anything else.

- State the why you are bringing this to the group.

- State any direct facts about this.

- State any history, events, timelines and/or connections to this with your organization, or any experience you personally have had with the thing you are bringing to the group and why it is important for the group to understand this.

- State any feelings you are having about this and why you are feeling this (fear, excitement, doubt, hesitation, optimism, pessimism, guilt, anger, distrust, happiness, etc.).

- State any supporting data you have about this.

- State any additional information the group should know.

- State exactly what questions you are asking to the group and how the group can help.

- State what outcomes you believe this could deliver or not deliver.

The request for information in the above format can be delivered in a written document presented on screen, in a handout format, on a slide deck, or verbally presented. It is advised at least to have a presentation and handouts so your peer performance group can take notes and dive in.

Note: Requests for information need to be completed ahead of time so group members have time to read them and consider suggestions or additional questions they may have before the group meets.

Once you have effectively delivered the request for information in the format above, it is time for the group to go around and give feedback. I recommend first doing this in a loose format, allowing members to chime in where they see fit. Then I do recommend the facilitator go round robin style and ask for any last advice.

Once the feedback has been delivered and no more questions have been posed by either the host who has presented the request for information or by the group, it is time for the host to validate what they heard from the group. The validation step is a critical step any time a round of feedback is given.

VALIDATION

Validation is the process by which the host, or any group member who is formally receiving feedback, delivers back the information they heard and their biggest takeaways from the round of feedback from the group. It is important for anyone that is receiving feedback to take handwritten notes. We are a big proponent of handwritten notes because physical note taking helps the mind comprehend and process information for the long-term memory. Validation helps the group member receiving the feedback organize their notes and make commitments to the group.

There is an important distinction between validation and goal setting. At the end of each peer performance group meeting, the group will set goals together and commit to those goals with each other. Validation is not goal setting. Validation is strictly asking the host to organize the most impactful feedback they heard from the group and recite it back to the group to ensure all feedback was understood.

At the end of each request for information, the facilitator should ask the host to validate what they heard. The host should read back the top 5-10 most impactful pieces of feedback they heard.

If there are multiple points of view or multiple opinions on a course of action or next step, the host may validate all of those points were heard. The group may want to further debate in depth the best course of action if multiple options were presented to the host. A SWOT (strengths, weaknesses, opportunities, threats) analysis or a simple pros & cons list can be created if this is the case. It is a good idea for the facilitator to ask the host if they would like to deep dive into the options presented before moving on to the next request for information. Or, if the host decides on one course of action, the host should state what exactly they are deciding to do, but thank the members for all of their input.

Validation allows the host to ensure each group member was heard, and to ensure all group members feel their point was delivered and well received. It confirms that the message being delivered was heard by the host in the right context.

DAY 3:
The peer presentations

The third day of the peer performance group meeting is for each individual member to present their material and gather feedback from the group. The interesting tendency, and often an unintended consequence of the format of this meeting, is the fact that while analyzing and giving feedback to the host about their organization, peer group members are also learning what they can do, and picking up improvements throughout the day during the host presentation. This phenomenon is an awesome side effect and will be prevalent in Day 3 of the meeting. Peer group members may come to the meeting with similar request for information presentations, and those questions may get answered during the host presentation. Peer group members may also come with questions or opportunities, and during the host presentation, a situation or opportunity may come up that is like other group member's, thus answers may be formulated during the host presentation. Nonetheless, the final day of the meeting is for each group member to present their information, and an equal amount of time is given for each member.

The agenda for the final day with the group will look like this:

- Individual presentations
  - o Data and financial presentations
  - o Request for information presentation
  - o Validation
- Working lunch (*this is a long day with lots to cover—we recommend a working lunch delivered in or prepared in advance*)
- Parking lot items (time permitting)
- Housekeeping
  - o Review format, any changes?
  - o Plan next meeting date and location.
  - o Requests for or questions about food, lodging, activities.
  - o This is where anything else goes for discussion.
- S.M.A.R.T. goal setting & check out
  - o How are you feeling?
  - o Top three takeaways
  - o Three to five S.M.A.R.T. goals you would like to accomplish before the next group meeting (peer groups will hold you accountable and you will report on these goals at the beginning of each meeting)
- Adjourn for flights out or downloading/unwinding quiet time

THE INDIVIDUAL PRESENTATIONS:
PART 1 – COMPARING DATA

The individual presentations are going to be similar in form and fashion to the host presentation but broken down into a shorter presentation. It is recommended that each presenter have at least one and a half hours, preferably two hours. However, as you can see, if you have six group members and five are scheduled to present on Day 3, that will equal 10 hours of presentations if each member gets two hours. It's a good idea to format your peer group presentation day based on how many group members are in the group. For larger groups, it is optional to hold peer group presentations on arrival day, after the host presentation is over, or add an additional day to the group meeting as to not rush the peer group presentations.

The peer group presentation consists of sharing data such as financials, growth metrics, business key performance indicators, and market data. It is important to work as a group to compare data in similar formats (as similar or the exact same data if possible). This will allow group members to challenge each other on areas of improvement and see where a certain member is strong or weak. It is also important to share data within the same time ranges as each other. For example, if the meeting is in November, all group members may agree to share three quarters' worth of data. Thus, the financial statements, marketing metrics, or whichever key performance indicators you decide to share, would represent January 1st – September 30th.

The same goes for comparing time periods in the same organization. It is important when sharing data to compare the same time periods for years past. For example, if I was showing financial data, instead of showing one year from January 1st – September 30th, I may choose to show the previous two years of that same period. In this I will be able to share with the group our growth as well as cost of expansion and, thus, improved or lack of profitability. It is imperative to note that when sharing and comparing profit and loss statements, it is critical to share two reports: a summary report that is more condensed and a detailed report which shows each line of the statement. Always show actual dollar figures and percentages of revenue. Group members may not have comparable profit and loss statements, but when comparing summary statements and looking at percentages of revenue, group members can observe opportunities and ask smarter questions.

Groups that operate in the same business or in the same organization (i.e., franchisees, franchisors, small business owners in the same trade but different cities, or non-profit organizations) will want to map data side by side to allow for easy comparison. Mapping data simply means putting each group member's data on a spreadsheet side by side so that comparisons can be made easily, and discussions can be had. By doing so, the group can dive deeper into who is strong in what areas of their business and who has room for improvement. This is a great tool for group members to fine tune their businesses and learn from each other.

On top of mapping financial data, as part of housekeeping and as groups grow together, you will want to discuss at least five metrics or data points the group members all have in common and to map them on the same spreadsheet or graph before each meeting. As groups mature, this list grows to 10 or more key performance indicators group members are sharing at each meeting. These can include sales metrics, costs ratios, social media and digital marketing campaign comparisons, customer response and market data, donor data, or any other key performance indicator the group feels would be important to compare. It will vary widely by industry and group.

THE INDIVIDUAL PRESENTATIONS:
PART 2 – THE REQUEST FOR INFORMATION

By now you have read plenty about the request for information and how the format works based on the host presentation. Each peer performance group member is allotted one request for information, and based on amount of time, or if they get their first one answered during the host presentation, they may choose to skip to a second one they have one prepared. For a full description of the request for information format, refer to the host presentation day section. As a quick reference, here are the questions and the format to be followed for the request for information presentation.

The request for information should be executed in this order:

- State the opportunity, challenge, hunch, position or person to be discussed, issue, or anything else.

- State the why you are bringing this to the group.

- State any direct facts about this.

- State any history, events, timelines and/or connections to this with your organization, or any connection you personally have had with the thing you are bringing to the group and why it is important for the group to understand this.

- State any feelings you are having about this and why you are feeling this (fear, excitement, doubt, hesitation, optimism, pessimism, guilt, anger, distrust, happiness etc.).

- State any supporting data you have about this.

- State any additional information the group should know.

- State exactly what questions you are asking to the group, and how the group can help.

- State what outcomes you believe this could deliver or not deliver.

VALIDATION

At the end of each peer performance group presentation group members will go around and provide additional feedback or state anything that was not delivered during the peer performance group members time sharing. At the end of each peer presentation, it is important to ask the presenter to validate what they heard and what were the big takeaways. This is how each presenter will end their presentation, and it will determine the start of the next presentation. It is a good idea to take a quick stretch break in between each presentation.

PARKING LOT

After all peer member presentations have been presented, the end of the meeting is approaching, but some of the most important parts of the meeting have yet to be executed. The parking lot represents an opportunity to review relevant information, discussions, or debates that the facilitator has decided are strong topics, but did not want the group to steer off course during the meeting. A strong meeting facilitator will utilize the parking lot as an area for ideas to be "parked" when a conversation is going off on a tangent. Often group members may engage in separate conversations or a side conversation may emerge—if that is the case, we can interrupt the side conversation and ask if the discussion needs to be added to the parking lot. This is also a great tool, and less invasive way, to end a side conversation.

Depending on the number of parking lot items, it is advised to allow at least 30 minutes to an hour to discuss all items on the parking lot.

To get started, it is a good idea to have someone read and summarize all items on the parking lot. Often, issues will have "died on the vine" or are no longer relevant and can be crossed off. There will likely be some hot topics that will rise to the top and members will agree are the highest priority to be discussed first. If all parking lot items are not able to be addressed based on time, it is a good idea to address them on a conference call shortly after the meeting, or a plan of action or owner of each parking lot item should be assigned prior to leaving the meeting.

HOUSEKEEPING

Once all parking lot items have been addressed, it is time to review housekeeping items. The facilitator should review and discuss the following items.

Is the format clearly understood by all and do all group members agree with the current format of the meeting? Do any changes need to be made? Do we need an extra day or an earlier mandatory arrival time? Do we need a mandatory later departure time? These are all good questions to review with the group to ensure everyone understands the format of the meeting and is aligned with the why and how the group will execute each meeting going forward.

Housekeeping is a good opportunity to ask all members if they agree their time and money invested to be a part of the group was worth it, and if they will be returning. If they are hesitant, ask what are their hesitations? What can the group do to make their investment more valuable and their time spent with the group stronger? These open and honest conversations at the end of each meeting truly help bond and align groups for longer lasting relationships and collaboration.

Do group members believe any other members need to be added? If so, who or how will the group go about recruiting new members? Are there any members who are struggling with attendance? If so, what course of action should be taken? Do bylaws need to be implemented, or does the group feel attendance issues should be addressed on a one-off basis? These are all items that should be reviewed after each meeting.

When will the next meeting take place and at what location? Ask all group members to open their calendar applications, or write down two dates that may be great meeting dates for the next host. As the facilitator, you do not have to lock down next meeting dates at this meeting, but make sure to get two dates or two weeks that work for all. The next host, or the group facilitator, will send out an email asking for confirmation again and then set a date. Typically, this is best completed two weeks after the meeting has taken place.

Are there any requests or modifications needed for food, lodging, or activities? This is a great time to discuss the next meeting and what will make it better. For a full list of applications to assist in finding meeting spaces and activities, see the appendix at the end.

Housekeeping is also the section where anything else can go that will need to be discussed. The facilitator has the choice to add items to the housekeeping list or the parking lot as needed.

THE CHECK-OUT AND S.M.A.R.T. GOAL SETTING

The check-out process is a process in which all groups should participate, and it allows the group members to share with each other their big takeaways and how they are feeling after the meeting.

The check-out also will allow each group member to assign themselves S.M.A.R.T. goals, for which they will report back to each other during the check-in at the next peer performance group meeting. The check-out consists of three questions:

- How are you feeling now (as opposed to before the meeting)?

- What are your top three to fifth takeaways from this meeting?

- What are your top three S.M.A.R.T. goals you wish to accomplish before the next group meeting?

S.M.A.R.T. goals are defined as simple, measurable, attainable, realistic, and timely. What does this mean?

- All smart goals must be simply defined in one sentence or phrase.

- Must have one measurable metric that will define success. How will you measure that this goal has been achieved? What's the metric to define the goal as completed? Or be specific about what needs to happen for this goal to be achieved.

- Must be attainable and realistic, considering resources, time, money, and technology.

- All goals must have a deadline. Must be defined by when they will be achieved.

The facilitator should ask members to read back their goals aloud to the entire group. If a goal is not specific enough or does not follow the above guidelines, the facilitator and group should encourage the member who is sharing to make the goal more specific. Group members and the facilitator can talk aloud with the member about how to make the goal more specific and in the above format, and when the entire group agrees that it is a S.M.A.R.T. goal, then the member may move on to the next goal. A strong facilitator will ask questions that will provoke the goals to get "smarter."

Facilitator questions for goal-setting sessions:

- How can we break that down to make it more bite-sized? (Make it simple.)

- What metric will you track regularly and how will you define when the goal is completed with this metric? (Make it measurable.)

- Do you have the resources to achieve this goal? If so, what are they?

- When will you have this goal achieved by?

HACKING GOALS: EASIER WAYS TO SET SPECIFIC AND SMART GOALS

We find often peer performance groups who are just flat out bad at setting goals that are specific, measurable, timely, and strong enough to be a top-three goal that the group is going to hold the goal setting member accountable for. To assist with facilitators and peer performance group members in setting specific goals that are going to be impactful, we put together a "Hacking Your Goals Question and Answer" guide to help. These are questions to complete when goal setting, and a facilitator can ask these verbally or use our "hack your goals" worksheet available for download at www.disruptfromwithinbook.com

Follow these steps to execute on extremely specific goals. Facilitators should guide the peer performance group members through these steps.

Step 1: Write down exactly how the goal came to you. Write down the goal unedited, and we will work it through the next few steps to make it specific and S.M.A.R.T.

Step 2: Write down at least one accountability partner you will enroll in this goal to hold you responsible to the goal. This may or may not be a peer performance group member. This may be multiple people including colleagues, peer performance group members, friends, or family.

Step 3: Write down key dates that you will report your progress to your accountability partner. Include next to each date if that will be a face-to-face meeting, a phone call, a lunch, a webinar, or a video chat. How will you report the progress to your accountability partner and on which days? These can be weekly, monthly, or quarterly check-ins. The person setting the goals should choose the check-in and update cadence.

Step 4: Write down how you will track your goal (spreadsheet, journal, whiteboard, software, application, etc.).

Step 5: Pick your measurable win. How will you know your goal is 100% completed? What will need to happen? What key metric will determine the goal is 100% completed? What action item has to happen or be performed that will deem the goal completed? For every goal, there is almost one metric or key performance indicator and an action item that deems the goal completed. Think hard here.

Optional: How will you reward yourself upon completion of this goal? How will you reward the team who achieves this goal if this is a team effort?

Step 6: Rewrite the goal in the following format:

My goal is to (accomplish, do, reach, excel, hit, execute):

_____

_____

_____.

I will start on this goal on _____ and my target date of completion for this goal is _____. My deadline to absolutely crush this goal is _____.

My accountability partners that I will enroll in this goal are _____ and _____. I will report my progress on this goal on _____, _____, _____ and _____. I will report my progress with my accountability partners on the above days by this method: _____.

I will track my goal, and provide access to my accountability partners to my goal tracking by using _____.

The key performance indicator I will use to track my goal is _____.

The goal for the above metric is _____. When my goal is 100% completed, the metric will reflect this number.

The actions or events that need to happen as a result of hitting the goal above are:

_____

_____

_____.

Optional: I will reward myself, or my team, when I achieve my goal with

_____

_____

_____.

Congratulations! You have written an extremely specific goal or have coached your peers on how to make their goals S.M.A.R.T. Good luck!

Note: Peer performance groups should keep each round of goal setting in the same database or document. It is great to go back and reflect on achievements made throughout the lifetime of the peer performance group.

ADJOURN

After the check-out process, all members will have had time to state their goals and final words for the group before adjourning. The facilitator should say any parting words or discuss any logistics, but some group members (if not the entire group) may elect to depart the day after the peer performance group presentations. We find this "download time" or "winding down time" allows for group members to relax before heading back to their organizations, outline their notes, and start to draft plans on how they will enact their takeaways.

CHAPTER 6:
Keeping it fresh and adding even more value, year after year.

One of the biggest challenges of a peer performance group is continuing to provide value to each group member throughout the life of the group. Some groups, or some group members, do not struggle with this at all, as the group dynamic continues to push and build over time. Many groups over the years begin to not only see the value in having an accountability team in place, but also see extreme value in the friendships formed and the entrepreneurial therapy that takes place during each peer performance meeting. However, many peer performance groups have an opportunity to continue to add in extra activities and development exercises to continue to drive accountability among the group—this helps improve each other's personal relationships as well as professional leadership skills.

Let's look at ten activities as a facilitator or peer performance group member that you can implement into your group meetings on years two through five to add additional value to the group. It is encouraged to go through the entire process discussed in this book and start with that process, but when the group may be looking for more, these tools are here to help and add value. By no means do groups need to add any of these tools or events, and we encourage their use at the facilitator's discretion and absolutely not all at once during one meeting.

Many groups that decide to add in team building and personal development activities into their retreat add an additional day for these exercises and downloading into their agenda. As the maturity and the dynamic of the peer performance group continues to grow, groups will want to discuss how to incorporate these activities into their agenda.

#1 TEAM BEHAVIORAL FEEDBACK LOOP

In this exercise, peer performance group members will be asked to provide feedback about each other and directly deliver that feedback to each other in a round robin format. This exercise is for self-improvement as well as to improve self-awareness of each other. This exercise can be extremely impactful for not only developing each other's leadership abilities, but the practice of delivering feedback among group members naturally bonds the group further and improves trust and transparency.

This exercise originated from Patrick Lencioni's book, *Overcoming the Five Dysfunctions of a Team: a Field Guide.*

This exercise will take up to two hours, depending on the size of the peer performance group, so it is a good idea to schedule this into the retreat agenda ahead of time.

This simple but effective exercise takes place in three steps.

Step 1: Have one member volunteer to go as the first to receive feedback. Ask each team member to answer the following questions, on a blank piece of paper, quietly first by writing them down, and then the group will go around and share each other's feedback to the person who volunteered to go first to receive the feedback.

- What is that person's top communication style or behavioral characteristic that contributes to the strength of the team or to the strength of their organization?
- What is that person's top communication style or behavioral

characteristic that detracts from the strength of the team or the strength of their organization?

Step 2: Once all team members have finished answering the two questions above and have agreed they all have finished writing their answers, start by asking each person to share both of their answers.

Step 3: Ask the person receiving the feedback to record the top takeaways they receive or keywords they hear from each person.

Step 4: Ask the person who has received the feedback to validate what they heard by reading back the keywords and key takeaways or patterns that they heard for both questions. This is an incredibly reflective exercise that not only gives the person receiving the feedback behavioral areas to work on, but also identifies strengths they should continue to exemplify and even double down on.

Step 5: Repeat the entire process above for each group member.

The above exercise is a great team-building exercise that will leverage the group dynamic and provide each peer performance group member with constructive feedback to work on, as well as validate for them their strengths and areas of opportunity to work on. We recommend doing this exercise annually and keeping a record of the feedback each year. By doing so, group members can reflect on their behavioral characteristics and feedback given each year, and determine where they have improved the most and where they still have room for improvement.

#2 ON THIS DAY EXERCISE

In this exercise we are going to write a story about what the business or organization looks like exactly five years from now and share the exact vision with each peer performance group member. Group members are also encouraged to assist each other in getting the stories as specific as possible and to encourage each member to set big dreams and visions.

The purpose of this exercise is for group members to realign with each other after spending time together and getting to know each other's organizations for at least one year. The realignment exercise allows group members to support each other in thinking big. It allows group members to engage with each other's goals. Often, after a year of peer performance support, goals and visions may change. Now is the time for members to rewrite a goal or vision and think bigger with the support of their peers.

Step 1: Imagine each group member is writing a news headline five year from now. As a group, each member is not going to write their exact news article for the five-year vision, but each person will write a headline and key points. Thus, this step involves writing the five-year vision headline describing their organization, their big accomplishment, or big event they are announcing.

Step 2: Write down three to five key elements that will be described in the article. Be as descriptive as possible about each of the elements. Describe the who, what, how many, how it was achieved, the effort that was needed, and the overall outcome of the event. Describe the community, the people involved, and the look and feel of each element.

Step 3: To finish the exercise, have each member write out a final statement describing what's next after this period, and describing an even bigger vision, an extra three to five years outside of this initial press release. This final step will encourage each person completing the exercise to think even bigger and share those even bigger dreams with the group.

This exercise is a great way for group members to align with each other's dreams and goals. It is incredibly impactful to add to a third day of meetings after group members are feeling supported and have spent two days analyzing and building momentum together. The group will collectively push each other to dream bigger and share those big goals. We highly encourage this exercise at least once annually.

#3 LEVERAGE THE NETWORK WITH GUEST SPEAKERS

Another great addition to kick off or end a meeting is to have guest speakers join the meeting and provide insights, stories, and educational opportunities. Ask each peer performance group member to list out at least five mentors, business leaders, or friends and family members that they believe would bring value, entertainment, and provide the group with takeaways. Guest speakers allow for group members to ask questions and get an outside perspective on challenges they are facing. Guest speakers with stories of failure and overcoming obstacles to success make for great motivational storytellers and help propel momentum created from the peer performance group.

To start gathering information about potential guest speakers, facilitators are encouraged to ask each member to spend 10 minutes in quiet time during a break or a scheduled time to write down the name, organization, title, phone, and email address for at least five people they believe would make for great guest speakers at the next peer performance group meeting.

#4 SPECIALTY SKILLS TRAINING FOR DEVELOPMENT OR ENTERTAINMENT

Another great way to encourage team collaboration or collectively grow together as a peer performance group is to enroll in a specialty skills training event together, or hire an expert to work with the entire group during the meeting. These can be anything related or completely unrelated to the background or the industry of the group, but we have provided a list to get you started.

1. Private cooking lessons

2. Time management skills course

3. Meditation training and beginner meditation exercises

4. Productivity hacks and technology hacks to improve productivity

5. Escape rooms and puzzle rooms for team collaboration

6. Beginning language education for a second language

7. An introduction to coding or computer technology/IT

8. Professional painting or drawing lessons

9. Yoga instruction or stretching instructions

10. Personal health consulting, dietitian consulting, or physical fitness and personal heath testing

#5 THE WHEEL OF LIFE BALANCE ASSESSMENT

This exercise is well known around the self-help community, and it's one that is executed in many groups and utilized by growth coaches worldwide. It is a great exercise to slow down the business or leadership mindset of group members and take a bird's eye view of their entire life, where it is currently. This tool is great for facilitators who want to add more value to the overall benefit of being in a peer performance group. Here are the steps to execute the Wheel of Life exercise:

Step 1: Have group members look at each area of their life and circle or write in a score from 1 to 10 in each area—10 meaning, "I feel totally great and satisfied with this area of my life" and a 1 meaning, "I feel totally broken in this area and this area needs tremendous improvement and attention."

Step 2: Once all members agree that they all have completed the wheel for where they are right now in their life, each member should reflect on three areas they would like to improve upon. Have them write the three areas down in the blank space under the wheel.

Step 3: For the three areas chosen by each group member, have them write first, what score they would like to move the specific category to by the date of the next meeting, and second, how they will move the score to that improved score. What exactly will they do? Who will they enroll to help them? What action needs to happen to move that score? Have group members record exactly what they will do next to each category and the number that they desire to be at in this area.

Step 4: Ask each member to share with the team their top three areas that they selected. Ask them to start out by sharing where they are now, where they want to improve their score to by the next meeting with the group, why they want to improve that area, and what they plan to do or what action items they have to take to improve that score.

Step 5: Encourage group members to share experiences and provide encouragement, and also encourage group members to share progress at each meeting by sharing the Wheel of Life exercise from the previous meeting and re-evaluating each meeting.

Below you will find the Wheel of Life exercise, and you may also visit www.disruptfromwithinbook.com/bonus to download the exercise in handout format and additional bonus material:

WHEEL OF LIFE EXERCISE

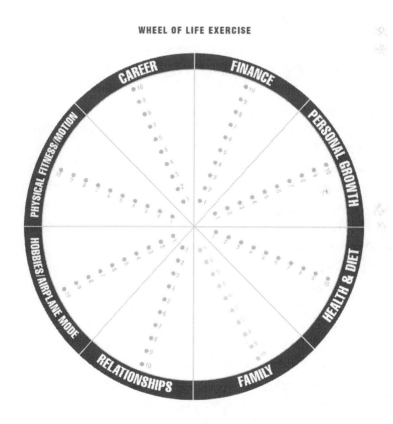

#6 THE DO WHAT YOU LOVE EXERCISE

The Do What You Love exercise is a great exercise to do at every meeting. And compare notes from the members' previous meetings. This simple, yet extremely powerful exercise will take a look at everything your members do on a daily, weekly, and monthly basis, and look for areas of opportunity to delegate and refocus. One of the most valuable roles a leader can add to their business is any role that will execute on tasks or projects that the leader is not skilled in doing, the leader does not love doing, or is not in line with the value the leader brings to the organization or the compensation they are asking. The most common insight this exercise delivers is the need for administrative support or sales support. However, many times, leaders do not know where to start or what to offload in order to fulfill the need for a full-time added role to their business. One important thing to note is that it does not need to be a full-time position. Check out the bonus in the middle of this book, to learn more about how to recruit and onboard a virtual team of help.

To start on this exercise, ask group members to start writing things down that they do every day or each week. Encourage members to think in detail, and really look down to each hour or each minute. As a pre-exercise, you may ask all members to journal for one week, prior to attending the meeting, what exactly they spend their time on. Are they doing administrative tasks, HR tasks, filing or emailing, promoting social media, selling, working on projects, or attending many meetings (noting the quantity), and whether they are necessary.

The goal of this exercise is simple, and the quadrant labels tell users exactly what to do. The X and Y axis of this chart will help group members determine where they should place each task, meeting, or project. On the X axis are things members love or hate. On the Y axis are tasks, meetings, or projects that members are skilled in or not skilled in, or they feel they bring little value to the task, meeting, or project.

Quadrant One will include tasks or projects that users absolutely should delegate immediately. Quadrant Four are tasks, projects, or meetings that should stay with the group member, and these are areas to remain focused on or do more of. Quadrants Two and Three are areas to reflect on and consider before delegating.

Next you will find the exercise, and you may also visit www.

disruptfromwithinbook.com/bonus to download the exercise in handout format and additional bonus material:

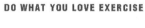

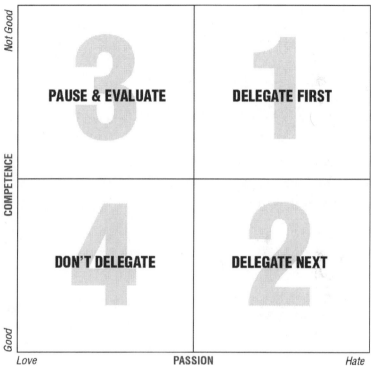

#7 MAP AND COMPARE EVEN MORE DATA — HERE IS A LIST:

SALES & MARKETING

- Number of opportunities to make a sale
- Number of leads
- Number of sales activities completed: presentations, proposals, meetings, pitches

- Closed business percentages/ratios
- Extra or add on sales – extra sales outside of the standard scope of business
- Expected revenue
- Actual revenue
- Performance metrics to budget – total revenue to budgeted revenue
- Cash to plan or cash to budget
- Expense to plan as a percentage
- Raw percentages of expenses (compare each businesses labor cost comparable to revenue)
- Digital marketing metrics: cost per click, cost per lead, cost per client acquisition

OPERATIONS

- All variable costs metrics and costs to produce one-unit ratios to revenue or sales per unit
- Errors and cost of errors, or claims or cost to satisfy a customer claim
- Waste or warranty comparable to sales
- Customer satisfaction rating or net promoter score (Listen360 is a great company to execute this metric)
- Average hourly rate to produce
- Direct labor cost versus production or revenue generated

FINANCE

- Weekly, monthly, or annual revenue
- Cash balance versus budget, performance, or cash to plan
- Accounts receivables and timelines of those accounts

- Gross profit margin – even better if all variable expenses are determined to be the same for all organizations

- Net profit margin

- Employee satisfaction rating (Tiny Pulse is a great firm to execute this metric)

- Open positions

- Payroll costs versus production

#8 ADD A BUSINESS CHECKUP – SELF-AUDIT AMONG THE GROUP

Another great way to add value to your peer performance group is to add a group audit or self-audit to execute together in a group setting, or each owner executes on themselves and reports back their findings to the group. We find adding the group audit to the peer performance host presentation day can elevate the presentation and can provoke more constructive and objective feedback for hosts. A group audit is also great for groups who are in the same or similar industries, or for business owners of the same business but who are not geographical aligned or not doing business in each other's markets.

A business checkup also serves as a long-term tool to measure progress. One of the most critical aspects of a business checkup is to execute the checkup, document and analyze what is missing, and then select what needs to be improved upon strategically. Peer performance group members who execute the business checkup either in a self-audit format or in a group setting will be inclined to want to execute on all the findings or all of the issues. The most important thing to think about is how to prioritize the opportunities found in the business checkup. Peer performance group members should utilize the power of the group to help each other prioritize the opportunities found in the business checkup and to develop a strategy on how to execute the opportunities identified after the checkup is completed.

The last but not certainly the least powerful benefit that a business checkup or audit tool will bring to your peer performance group is the ability of the group to identify weakness patterns and strength outliers among group members.

WHAT IS A WEAKNESS PATTERN?

A weakness pattern is an area of the business checkup that all or most group members are lacking or feel they are weak in. Once a weakness or pattern is identified, future initiatives for the group can be put into place. The group may decide to bring in a guest speaker that specializes in that topic, a training tool or consultant, or may decide to seek out another advisor or business that is particularly strong in that topic and spend time or visit with that owner or business.

WHAT IS A STRENGTH OUTLIER?

A strength outlier is an area of strength for one or the minority of the peer performance group members. When you identify the strengths of each peer performance group member's organizations, you can collectively identify the biggest opportunities for the other group members. It is critical to capitalize on the strengths of each group member and their organizations, so if groups identify what each of the other members are strong in, groups can begin to work on each other's organizations in those areas that are weak compared to those areas that are strong. This is the collective "high tides rise all ships" analogy, and this is precisely how this phenomenon happens.

THE DISRUPT FROM WITHIN BUSINESS FITNESS TEST

Utilize this test to identify areas of opportunity in each organization. Many of the questions are vague, so it is a good idea to not only check off (or not check off) each area, but to also add notes in the margins of the checklist where you see fit. The checklist is organized by organizational area; however, it may be skipped through or omitted as members see fit.

The Disrupt From Within Business Strength Assessment
Users should answer each question with a Yes or a No.
If it isn't a "hell yes," then it is a no.

CULTURE, RETENTION, & RECRUITING:

1. Our organization has one person or a committee responsible for driving culture and keeping culture a high priority by maintaining a cadence of quarterly team outings and culture building activities.

2. We use a tool to survey or check the regular pulse of culture by asking our team members to answer anonymous questions about workplace culture and grade the environment of the workplace.

3. We have a system in place to discuss the core values of the company on a daily basis and how team members have lived each core value.

4. We have regularly scheduled reviews with our team members for which we ask input on how leadership can improve and how we can improve the workplace.

5. We develop a career path plan and a personal goals plan for each of our team members and review that plan quarterly to ensure expectations and goals are being met for our team members on both a professional and personal level.

6. Our team members can easily recite our core values and our mission.

7. The three-year vision of the organization is shared by all, not just with all, and all team members can describe that vison.

8. We have one person assigned to the first point of contact for anyone entering our organization virtually or physically. That person lives and breathes our core values and is extremely passionate and personable.

9. We are always recruiting for top talent, even when we do not have open roles. We are building our bench of candidates who would fit in our organization that we can call upon at any time. We are always recruiting.

10. We have budgeted for personal and professional development for our team members. We regularly encourage our team members to participate (and they do) in leadership and team building as well as educational activities, courses, and seminars.

11. We have automated the employee recognition process including their anniversary, birthdays, spouse's and kids' birthdays. We send cards and gifts to their homes to recognize these occasions.

12. We provide fringe benefits to our team members to include things like gym memberships, house cleaning services, meal delivery, dry cleaning services, or style consulting subscriptions.

MARKETING & SALES:

1. We have clearly defined our target market and our customer profile, selecting a niche to go after, and our marketing efforts reflect that target market.

2. Our customer profile is understood by all in the organization.

3. Our marketing team has taken our annual revenue goal and reverse engineered a plan to drive the number of leads we need to hit that revenue goal—the team has developed a written plan to where those leads will come from and what percentage of the needed leads will come from each source.

4. We have a pre-defined marketing budget based on the number of leads needed above, and we regularly review the marketing budget and ROI from each marketing source.

5. We have an automated solution for gathering customer feedback and net promoter score. We utilize our net

promoter score and customer feedback to improve performance and share that feedback with all in the organization.

6. The organization has an automated loyalty and appreciation
program to send to clients on their anniversary, as well as
seasonal promotions to encourage repeat and referral.

7. Our clients receive incentive and recognition for referring
business, and we have automated this system.

8. We maintain a customer relationship management system
which automatically triggers touch point reminders for
customer and prospective follow ups. We regularly review
this system, and our sales-facing team members use this
system by implementing notes when touching base with
prospects and entering new prospects into the system.

9. We have clearly defined market differentiators, and our
entire team can recite those differentiators when speaking to
prospective clients. We also have a script of 5-10 questions
we ask all prospective clients before we discuss our business
or organization to avoid amateur sales vomiting.

10. Our entire organization can recite our 30-second or less
elevator pitch.

11. We review our brand imaging annually with outside
consulting and peer groups to determine if our imaging is
portraying our values, vision, and core business model. We
also seek feedback on any outdated material or any brand
imaging that may need to be refreshed. Our marketing
messages are up to date, modern, and bold.

OPERATIONS:

1. Our company's processes are documented in a manual with
standard operating procedures being listed and housed in
one place. This can be a simple one-page process for every
reoccurring task or procedure the organization does. If it
is a task or project that happens more than once per day,

once per week, or once per month, then it needs a standard operating procedure documented and filed. This can also be completed with video or screen casting and/or a hybrid of both.

2. Our onboarding of new team members and training exercises are documented and filed in the standard operating procedures.

3. Our operations team has a method of tracking and documenting progress that is reviewed by all on a weekly basis.

4. Our operations team reviews the costs of goods of the business and understands their budgets for projects or ongoing business.

5. We hold a daily huddle led by the culture team or operations team to review the day's accomplishments and good news.

6. We regularly secret shop ourselves and our competition to review how we did as well as how our competition is meeting or exceeding our client's expectations.

7. We regularly train and retrain our customer-facing team members on improving and gaining new service based skillsets.

8. We vet and review our vendor partners with whom we are doing business, and we look to outsource areas of the business that may be able to be completed cheaper, faster, or easier than us completing them in-house. We review at least two vendor partners or partner categories per quarter.

9. We review our per-unit production and variable costs annually and look for areas of improvement to drive gross profits. Our operations team is bonused or has incentives to drive higher gross profits on a quarterly basis. We review the gross profit on projects with our operations team.

10. Our operations team revisits our core business model and

our customer deliverables annually. We evaluate what is working and what isn't working, what issues our customers are facing, and how we can address those issues. Then we revisit the core business model. We do this by surveying our front-line team members and our customers to understand where we can improve and "wow" the end user.

FINANCE:

1. The leadership team and ownership receive regular and accurate financial statements to review by the 10th day of each month for the previous month.

2. The organization has access to capital via a line of credit or an operating account that contains at least two months of average payroll plus one month of fixed expenses available today.

3. A monthly summary of the financial health and profitability of the organization as well as cash flow is shared with the team.

4. A regular system or application of expense tracking by project and by team member for purchases and expenditures is in place.

5. The organization sets not just sales goals but net income goals annually and reviews those goals monthly in a performance report which includes actual versus budgeted revenue lines and expenses lines. We review the strengths and findings of this report with the entire team monthly.

6. The company sets cash flow targets and tracks those cash targets for the operating account. We discuss regularly how to improve cash flow and where our cash is spent to the entire team.

7. Our entire organization understands our breakeven point each month and understands when deciding to add a cost to

the organization, how much that will increase the breakeven point.

8. We review our invoices sent out and accounts receivable regularly to ensure clients are paying on time and we do not have outstanding balances due.

9. The organization meets with a qualified Certified Professional Accountant to discuss cash flow strategies and paying taxes. If taxes are to be owed, we make quarterly estimates and pay taxes quarterly to avoid big cash flow drains at each tax season.

10. We budget for and regularly participate in giving back to our community. When the company financially gains, the community gains, and we have this program written and planned ahead of time.

DATA & STATISTICS:

1. Everyone in the organization has at least one measurable or metric that defines their role. They have access to these metrics and review them with their leadership at least once per week.

2. We are a data-driven company—we use data to determine next steps, and we set goals and new initiatives with data included. When evaluating the success of a new client, project, or initiative, we look to the data first.

3. The organization has at least five metrics that are reviewed weekly that represent the core processes of the business.

4. Each business area has a core set of metrics to define the success of each initiative and task. The core metrics are reviewed by the business area leaders weekly, and the entire leadership team monthly.

5. We have assigned one person with the task of ensuring all data needed is collected in a timely manner, organized,

visualized, and displayed or sent to those who need to see the data.

LEADERSHIP ORGANIZATIONAL CHART & ACCOUNTABILITIES:

1. Our leadership organizational chart and business area organizational charts are clearly defined and available to be seen by all.

2. Each role in our organization has a clearly defined mission and accountabilities that are reviewed with each person fulfilling that role quarterly. If the mission or accountabilities are changed during that review, they are quickly updated.

3. Before we hire for any new role, the leadership team clearly defines the mission and accountabilities with all involved with that specific role, and those are published prior to posting or recruiting.

4. Our leadership team has access to and regularly meets with mentors and advisors to improve their respective business areas and the overall quality of their leadership.

5. Each member of the leadership team has three to five initiatives each quarter he or she is directly responsible for to move their business area and the organization further.

6. Together the leadership team has three to five annual initiatives they have agreed to accomplish for the year, and each one of those has an owner that is not specifically to be completed by that person, but the owner is responsible for seeing that initiative to completion.

IT & INNOVATION:

1. The organization has in-house or outsourced technical support for software and hardware, and access to that support is quick and easy to obtain.

2. If the organization has an in-house IT team, the team is

guided by a one-year roadmap which states the technology needs of the organization and the creation and onboarding schedule of these needs.

3. For all new technology, software, or IT processes added or modified, we adopt or create a standard operating procedure.

4. For all new technology, software, or IT processes added or modified, we assign an onboarding and adoption coach to that initiative.

5. We measure adoption and usage and add this metric to our dashboard until we feel the technology is fully adopted.

6. We complete a quarterly subscription and technology audit on all of our subscription-based technology and physical technology to confirm we are using the services and software and that the technology is in good physical order and up to date.

7. We schedule disruption days or innovation storms annually to disrupt our business model from within the business.

8. We assign team members to attempt to break our business model or our technology so we do not get complacent with our existing business and technology solutions. This team is rewarded when they discover opportunities to improve.

CLARITY & BALANCE: (LOOKING INWARD AT THE LEADER OF THE ORGANIZATION)

1. As the leader of the organization, I schedule clarity breaks to go quietly and think about growth of the organization and to plan and address current issues and challenges.

2. As the leader of the organization, I schedule and execute airplane modes to unplug and recharge my internal batteries for the health of my organization and my family.

3. As the leader of the organization, I schedule and execute on opportunities to grow professionally in my industry and

leadership by attending educational events and leadership development courses.

4. The organization and myself as the leader of the organization are supported by a board of advisors, board of directors, or peer performance group who hold me accountable to achieve the goals I set out to achieve.

5. I journal or write daily, weekly, monthly, and quarterly goals to reflect on progress and keep myself in focus.

6. I execute a morning routine that allows me to focus on myself and my mental, physical, and spiritual well-being before starting the workday.

HEALTH, MOTION, & DIET: (LOOKING INWARD AT THE LEADER OF THE ORGANIZATION)

1. As a leader of my organization or team, I regularly eat three meals per day including breakfast with limited sugar in all three meals.

2. As the leader of my organization or team, I regularly hold and invite team members to walking meetings. I try to walk for 15 minutes per day around the outside of the office or around town to provide more clarity.

3. I participate in a form of exercise with motion, stretching, or physical activity that raises my heart rate for 30 minutes, three times per week.

4. I weight train or resistance train at least one time per week.

5. I take at least one half day off per seven-day week to unplug from electronics and screens and spend time with family, in a quiet space, or with a hobby.

SUPPORT, ADVISORS, & MENTORS:

1. The organization has an assigned group of professional advisors to assist in the following areas, who are on-call and available at any time: legal, HR, insurance, IT, and accounting/taxes.

2. As a leader of the organization, I search out and regularly meet with mentors in a one-on-one setting who have succeeded in areas or have worked in businesses that have exceeded in areas that I am seeking for the organization. (We recommend 10-20 mentors in a leader's network with whom a meeting two to four times per year should take place.)

3. As the leader of the organization, I participate in a peer performance group of like-minded individuals and meet with this group at least three times annually. This group is my trusted group of advisors, and I set aggressive goals for which I am held accountable by this group.

4. I encourage and enroll the organization's leadership team in peer performance groups to inspire them to grow as individuals and leaders as well as be held accountable to goal set each year. This will allow our leaders to have a sounding board when facing issues and challenges.

5. To continue the mentorship cycle and to give back to the community, as the leader of the organization, I mentee individuals in the community or participate in volunteer efforts such as Big Brother and Big Sister groups.

VISION, MISSION, VALUES, AND BHAG (BIG HAIRY AUDACIOUS GOAL, FROM JIM COLLINS' GOOD TO GREAT):

1. As the leader of the organization, I have created the three-year vision for the organization in detail, including the look and feel of the organization, community involvement, roles and people in the business, and metrics and revenue targets.

That three-year vision is displayed for all to see and read. It is mandatory for all stakeholders to read including new candidates for roles in the organization, all team members, vendor partners, and advisors.

2. We revisit the three-year vision every year to ensure we are on track to achieve the vision, and every three years we rewrite this vision.

3. Our organization has a big hairy audacious goal that is posted for all to see and shared by the leader of the organization for all to understand.

4. As the leader of the organization, I share the core values and the mission of the organization with all stakeholders of the organization. It is my role to share the values, the mission, and the vision at any given chance.

5. Our leadership team regularly starts weekly planning meetings and quarterly review meetings by asking for stories and examples of how team members have lived the values and the mission of the organization.

MEETING RHYTHMS:

1. The organization's leadership team and each team within the organization meets weekly. This meeting consists of updating last week's goals, the current week's critical tasks, relevant metrics, and why they are or are not on target. During this meeting, the teams also address issues or challenges the team is facing, and attempts to resolve those challenges. *These meetings typically last 90-120 minutes each week.*

2. The organizational leadership team as well as individual business area teams participate in quarterly planning meetings. In these meetings, teams review the mission, values, vision, and last quarter's goals, and they set new goals based on the company's annual goals and one-year strategic plan. *These meetings typically last one full day,*

and we recommend professional facilitation for executive leadership planning meetings.

3. The organizational executive leadership team meets annually offsite for a two-day intensive deep dive and team-building event. This meeting is to review the annual goals from the existing year and set initiatives and goals for the next year. The team should review the mission and values and provide examples of how they have lived these core values. The team should review short-term wins for next year as well as large initiatives. The contents of the new year's planning session may come from the disruption sessions held earlier in the year. *This meeting should be two days long, include team building and planning, and we recommend professional facilitation.*

4. In meetings we focus on reviewing our core values, building trust and accountability, analyze core metrics for each role of the organization, and allow for deep discussion around challenges and issues team members are facing.

The above business assessment is intense and not for the faint of heart. Users should take their time when evaluating their business and take notes on each step. Areas marked "no" or "needs improvement" should then be shared with peer performance groups and added as takeaways and goals to be reported back to the group during the next meeting. It is also a strong tool for learning what other group members are executing on, and sharing how and with what tools they are executing in the areas other group members are not.

Facilitators can use the above business assessment tool to add to their host presentation day. This tool will add more depth to the host presentation, and usually after the second round of host presentations within a group, the actual presentation portion will be shorter, and the day will allow time for this assessment tool. By the time groups have met for one full round of a host presentation for each member, adding this tool will add a tremendous value to the host day. Also, revisiting this tool each year or each meeting will allow for improvement to be documented and new focus areas to be selected during each meeting.

#9 INTRODUCTION TO MEDITATION

Another way to add value to peer performance groups is by introducing meditation to group members. This exercise is more personal and for individual development, but meditation or the practice of taking breaks through therapy, music, silence, or going outdoors is something you'll find in the daily routine of almost all successful leaders.

In order to get started with meditation training, we recommend watching one or two introduction to meditation videos as a group, and then the facilitator can lead the group through one five-minute or one 10-minute session.

To get started with explaining and teaching the basics of meditation, we recommend the Headspace YouTube channel, and then after the peer performance group meeting adjourns, we recommend those who are interested in meditation download the Headspace app and execute the free 10-day meditation training. The first video on the Headspace YouTube channel will introduce meditation to the group and give the facilitator the groundwork for the one 10-minute meditation exercise.

Once all members have watched at least the introduction to meditation video by Headspace on YouTube, it's time to try meditation for the first time as a group. To do this, we are going to recommend facilitators start simple by asking members to meditate one minute at a time, and then reset by taking a deep breath, and then doing the same thing over again at least five times, with a maximum of ten times. Facilitators please explain the activity in whole before beginning. Let's get started.

Step 1: Have members sit on the floor, sitting up in comfortable clothing with no shoes on. Make sure the room is quiet and there are no distracting noises around including all devices which should be turned off or silenced.

Step 2: Explain to the group that we are going to close our eyes one minute at a time, and each minute the facilitator is going to announce the next minute by saying one, one, one, one, two, two, two, two, two slowly and with a low tone.

Step 3: Members are encouraged to sit still with their eyes closed for the entire minute, and once the minute is over and the facilitator announces the end of the minute, take a deep breath, open the eyes for a reset of one second, and then close them again and go into the next minute ready to meditate again.

Step 4: Ask members to meditate each minute and try to avoid any thoughts, or if thoughts arise, see them, observe them, but do not acknowledge them. Let them flow through the mind as if they are clouds passing on a windy day. With each minute that passes, the mind will begin to calm and group members will notice the advancement they are making in meditation by the mind gradually calming. With each new minute, less thoughts will try to be processed, and group members will become more skilled at not acknowledging their thoughts, rather allowing them to flow easily without acknowledgement.

Step 5: To finish this exercise, ask each group member to come out of meditation after the end of the fifth minute or the tenth minute, depending on how many minutes the group decides to do. At the end of the exercise, have each member share their experiences and thoughts during the first couple of minutes versus their experience and thoughts during the last few minutes. Members should be encouraged to share their mental state, what thoughts came into their minds, and how they felt after a slower minute. Did they see progress from the beginning of the exercise to the end of the exercise? What did they learn as the minutes progressed? The sharing portion will allow group members to learn from each other but also encourage them to get stronger at meditation through a daily practice.

To finish the exercise and encourage a daily mediation practice, we encourage group members to download the Headspace meditation app, sign up, and complete the free 10-day meditation training course.

#10 WHAT IS PEAK PERFORMANCE FOR ME? AN EXERCISE.

Many performance coaches, including the world-famous Tony Robbins, teach and talk about peak state and peak performance when describing world class athletes, artists, performers, musicians, and millionaires or billionaires. Peak performance or peak state is described when we are in "the zone." It is a mindset when we are at our best. A peak state can be a certain moment or time of day—it can be a period like months or days or somewhere in between.

As leaders of organizations, peer performance group members should spend time not just working on their organization's health, but members should also invest time in improving their own mental, physical, and spiritual state. This exercise will help focus on just that.

This is a great exercise for a group to learn more about each other, what motivates and drives each other, and it often will provide a jolt or idea to another member to help them obtain peak state or be in peak state for a longer period. This is a simple exercise where a facilitator will ask group members a couple of questions and group members will go around and share. Similar to the Wheel of Life exercise, this describes peak state for each member.

Step 1: Ask members to describe daily and weekly routines that happen when they are in peak state, or if they desire to be in their peak state, what is happening daily, weekly, and monthly.

Step 2: Describe routines that are happening regularly, or when these routines are happening, group members feel fulfilled and accomplished.

Step 3: Ask group members to describe what routines or areas of their life they want to increase in frequency, do more of, and those that will improve their peak state or get them into peak state more often.

Step 4: Have group members make a list of a list of their tasks, routines and activities, organized by daily, weekly, and monthly categories.

Step 5: Have group members share their lists as well as share what areas they want to improve upon or increase frequency of in order to maintain or increase their time in peak performance.

By asking members to share what each of their peak performance routines and activities include, members will give each other ideas and motivate each other. This will help the group keep doing what they are doing or make changes to their routine which in turn will help each other grow and improve together.

THE TOOLS OF "KEEPING IT FRESH"

The above tools represent 10 different activities facilitators can add to peer performance groups to add value and extend the agenda for group meetings. After host presentations have been executed for the entire group, and no new members have been added, it is a great idea to add one or two of these activities to the group each year. These will increase value, help the group continue to grow, and bring group members closer together creating an even stronger bond within the group.

Good luck!

APPENDIX:
Who can benefit from a peer performance group

For franchisees and franchise company executives: Peer performance group programs that are facilitated by franchise headquarter employees for groups of franchisees are one of the many reasons I love the franchise business model. The franchise business model is one of the most successful business models because of the ability to share data, best practices, marketing methods, and operational advantages. If you are a franchisee, and you are evaluating franchise business models to invest in, I would highly encourage you to ask about a peer performance group and how many franchisees take advantage of the program if there is one implemented. If you are a franchisor and do not have a peer performance group program, then you should consider forming groups for your franchisees, facilitated by support staff members or outside professional facilitation. A franchisee peer performance group program is an extremely valuable program which will drive franchisee engagement, growth, satisfaction and profitability. Justin Waltz offers training programs and facilitation of franchise mastermind programs. For more information please email JW@JustinWaltz.com.

For franchise executives: Peer performance groups in

franchising for franchise executives is a growing concept. There are plenty of business conferences and franchise conferences which allow for surface level information to be distributed to the group—these are great for development of your business and learning best practices. The International Franchise Association is a great association for learning the basics of franchising and how to handle the various issues that come with franchise growth. The next steps in true development of any franchise system is for the executives of the franchise brand to network and learn from other executives from other franchise brands. In order to do this, a peer performance group of franchise executives within the same scope of work from non-competing brands can be a highly impactful method to learn and grow, as well as learn what works and what doesn't work. These groups can be professionals from IT, Marketing, Operations, Franchise Development, Legal and Compliance, Accounting and Human Resources. Non-competing brands can come together to share data, financials, vendor networks, and best practices. I highly advise any rising franchise executive to discuss including a peer performance group into their compensation package as part of employment with any brand. This is a great way for anyone to propel their career, in any professional environment, not just franchising. There are franchise executive performance groups forming around the United States. For more info please email JW@JustinWaltz.com.

For small business owners in the same community (non-competing businesses): Small business owners in a community with different businesses make great peer performance group members. Every small business owner has a different background from the other. We all were raised differently, in different parts of the world, with different skillsets and different professional careers or journeys which got us to small business ownership. A group of individuals who can share stories and skillsets within the same community can impact success incredibly. There is also an opportunity to do cross-marketing together, co-op advertising, and expense sharing for community events.

For small business owners in the same industry or trade:

For business owners who have the same business, but in different, non-competing markets, this can be one of the biggest opportunities to grow your business from a revenue perspective and from a profitability perspective. I recommend recruiting members of the same business but in different markets from different states. The ability to travel and see other businesses will allow you to unplug and get away from your business and to also see how other businesses are running their operations by getting to add a tour of their business to the agenda. You will be able to compare data and financial statements which will show you areas of opportunity and areas that you are doing well in your business. I cannot highlight enough how impactful having a peer performance group of small business owners in the same business but in different markets can be to your growth. This will be a significant investment in your future and one that will pay off tenfold.

For professionals, executives, and entrepreneurs who have already achieve higher levels of success: If you have a level of support around you in the form of professional services (accountants or lawyers) plus executive level support (CFO, COO, CEO, CXO) then you are aware of the power of professional support and what that level of support can do for an organization. However, one of the most common complaints from CEOs and successful entrepreneurs is the lack of fulfillment in their daily lives. This is something a peer performance group can help with.

One way a peer performance group helps in fulfillment is by the practice of gratitude. As you can see in this book, we recommend a practice of gratitude, and recognizing what each group member is grateful for in each meeting, to add to the chemistry of the group but to also help build fulfillment. When gratitude appears, fear and negativity become diminished.

Fulfilment in the form of a peer performance group builds from within yourself, at different points of your group meetings and at different lifecycles of each group. At the beginning of each meeting, during the check-in, you lean into the group and state the things you are grateful for. This practice helps to not only eliminate negativity, but it also helps you share with the group what you have going on in your world. A great way to be more transparent to the group. It also helps group members point out even more things you have to be grateful for. Fulfilment can come in many forms, and oftentimes, fulfillment comes from the ability to share with others. At times, something one group member may be grateful for is something you may not have thought of but you are also grateful for. Now you are compounding fulfillment and gratitude in a group setting.

The next step in any journey to success is finding fulfillment. Helping others, sharing experiences, being vulnerable, and practicing gratitude is the first step to finding joy in your daily grind, and becoming more fulfilled with the path you have carved.

For non-profit organizations: A support group to share statistics, stories, marketing best practices, and struggles is so important for non-profit organizations. The best non-profit organizations are run with the same haste, urgency, and aptitude as a successful business, so go out there and find out who is doing what you want to do well, and then connect with them.

For coaches and league administrators: Coaches need coaches, and it goes a long way when coaches have coaches because it says you believe in coaching and it allows you to understand the impact coaching has on individuals. Coaches and league administrators of all sizes need to have a sounding board, away from parent organizations, to better understand how leagues perform, how coaches grow, and how to deal with issues when they do arise. It is extremely beneficial for coaches and league administrators to have a peer performance group to bounce ideas off of each other and to seek out advice from (away from parent groups, which at times, become biased based on the child's participation in the league and the politics of the league).

For sole proprietors of businesses and freelancers: Sole proprietors and freelancers have one of the toughest professions due to the singularity of the workplace and loneliness that comes with working for yourself. Personal trainers, photographers, therapists, freelance designers, and virtual assistants are just some examples of sole proprietors that need a peer performance group. A group can be compiled of people in the same trade or specific industry (or cross industry), but the issues and challenges that face sole proprietors can be very similar. It is a powerful exercise to have the ability to share data, marketing techniques, technology solutions, and just overall mental awareness with a group of sole proprietors. This is one reason we are seeing the rise of co-working spaces in every city in America; the natural mini-mastermind feel of co-working spaces are elevating those in them. These inspiring workspaces are creating peer performance groups unintentionally around the country. I love seeing co-working spaces buzzing with entrepreneurs feeding off each other's energy.

Human resource professionals, executive leadership and entrepreneurs: Please consider peer performance groups to be offered to be built into compensation packages. This is because organizations are always looking for additional non-monetary benefits to include in their benefits packages to differentiate their organizations. Consider including and encouraging the use of funds to join an existing peer performance group, or encouraging a team member to start one. The benefits could include the time to participate in the group, the flights, hotels and meals, and registration fees of the group. This is an incredible way to support your growing team and show that you believe in connecting them with industry professionals to continue their personal and professional development. Please consider this when creating your non-monetary benefits and bonus plans for your future team members.

For busy moms: Go find a new mothers' group or breastfeeding support group. It is so essential to have a sounding board of individuals who can support you in the journey of raising a newborn. It is so difficult sitting at home with a newborn—having a support group who you can speak with and share stories with is a great way to ensure success as well as keeping your sanity.

> *"Success without fulfillment is
> the ultimate failure."*
> *—Tony Robbins*

APPENDIX:
Benjamin Franklin's Junto – questions to start discussion:

These questions were written in the 1700s, thus language and context may not make sense, but we left them in their original form for historical representation.

1. Have you met with anything in the author you last read, remarkable, or suitable to be communicated to the Junto? Particularly in history, morality, poetry, physics, travels, mechanic arts, or other parts of knowledge?

2. What new story have you lately heard agreeable for telling in conversation?

3. Has any citizen in your knowledge failed in his business lately, and what have you heard of the cause?

4. Have you lately heard of any citizen's thriving well, and by what means?

5. Have you lately heard how any present rich man, here or elsewhere, got his estate?

6. Do you know of any fellow citizen, who has lately done a worthy action, deserving praise and imitation? or who has

committed an error proper for us to be warned against and avoid?

7. What unhappy effects of intemperance have you lately observed or heard? of imprudence? of passion? or of any other vice or folly?

8. What happy effects of temperance? of prudence? of moderation? or of any other virtue?

9. Have you or any of your acquaintance been lately sick or wounded? If so, what remedies were used, and what were their effects?

10. Who do you know that are shortly going [on] voyages or journeys, if one should have occasion to send by them?

11. Do you think of anything at present, in which the Junto may be serviceable to mankind? to their country, to their friends, or to themselves?

12. Hath any deserving stranger arrived in town since last meeting, that you heard of? and what have you heard or observed of his character or merits? and whether think you, it lies in the power of the Junto to oblige him, or encourage him as he deserves?

13. Do you know of any deserving young beginner lately set up, whom it lies in the power of the Junto any way to encourage?

14. Have you lately observed any defect in the laws, of which it would be proper to move the legislature an amendment? Or do you know of any beneficial law that is wanting?

15. Have you lately observed any encroachment on the just liberties of the people?

16. Hath anybody attacked your reputation lately? and what can the Junto do towards securing it?

17. Is there any man whose friendship you want, and which the Junto, or any of them, can procure for you?

18. Have you lately heard any member's character attacked, and how have you defended it?

19. Hath any man injured you, from whom it is in the power of the Junto to procure redress?

20. In what manner can the Junto, or any of them, assist you in any of your honorable designs?

21. Have you any weighty affair in hand, in which you think the advice of the Junto may be of service?

22. What benefits have you lately received from any man not present?

23. Is there any difficulty in matters of opinion, of justice, and injustice, which you would gladly have discussed now?

24. Do you see anything amiss in the present customs or proceedings of the Junto, which might be amended?

APPENDIX:
Questions to dive deeper in your off time

Use the following questions to dive deeper with group members in your office, over fire, or over a cocktail.

1. What's keeping you up at night?

2. What is your biggest challenge this year that will keep you from hitting your goals?

3. What position are you adding next, or who are you looking to promote to a leadership role, and what role?

4. Are you a reader? Non-fiction or fiction? If so, what book has really impacted you lately?

5. What did you learn today?

6. What surprised you today?

7. What was good to hear today or what was validating?

8. What stressed you out the most these days?

9. How do you relax?

10. Do you take clarity breaks? If so, how often? Where?

APPENDIX:
Top 10 ice breakers to open a meeting with vulnerability

1. So far, the most important decision in my life was/is…

2. If I suddenly found out that I had 24 hours to live, I would spend them…

3. What is your greatest fear in life?

4. What is your most treasured memory?

5. What do you want your legacy to be? What do you want your headstone to say?

6. What would you need to do to achieve your 10-year goal in six months or less?

7. What is the most surprising thing you are have learned about your childhood?

8. What gift, service, skill, or talent do you offer the world? Are you utilizing it now, if so, how?

9. What holiday has the most meaning to you? Why?

10. Who is the most significant person in your life? Why?

The four mindsets of every successful peer performance group

These are the four mindsets for creating lifeline relationships. In his book, *Who's Got Your Back: The Breakthrough Program to Build Deep, Trusting Relationships That Create Success and Won't Let You Fail,* Keith Ferrazzi outlines these four critical mindsets.

MINDSET #1: GENEROSITY

In his book, Ferrazzi outlines that it is almost impossible to be negative or be in a victim mindset when we are practicing generosity in our daily lives and also in our peer performance groups. Generosity can come in the form of helping others once we determine how we can serve them, and also it can come in the simplest form of connecting with another person and empathizing or caring for their situation.

Another important part of generosity is the ability to accept another person's generosity towards you, the receiver. In this book Ferrazzi states, "Whether we realize it or not, this willingness to 'give and let give' creates a wonderful give-and-take in a relationship."

MINDSET #2: VULNERABILITY

Vulnerability is one of the biggest character traits important to creating lifelong relationships, and Ferrazzi tells us that vulnerability is key. Vulnerability is the courage to show your fears, your struggles, and your inner thoughts and allow those around you to help. It requires you to admit your weaknesses and share exactly what you are thinking. Vulnerability also requires you to be proactive in your approach to building relationships. You do not have to be vulnerable—you must make the choice to practice vulnerability. This means admitting fault and fears, and opening up and presenting these to the group. Your inner circle may not proactively seek to go deeper with you until you reveal what exactly you are struggling with. However, when you do, you invite those around you to help you, and share with you. The beauty of vulnerability is that it's contagious in nature. The more vulnerable group members become with one another, the more others will open up. We will practice vulnerability in the meeting ice breakers and morning check-in. This is the perfect time to start practicing vulnerability, and we will share a list of ice breakers that help with vulnerability in the appendix of this book.

MINDSET #3: CANDOR

Candor is defined by the *Merriam-Webster Dictionary* as unreserved, honest, or sincere expressions. Keith Ferrazzi describes candor as the ability to engage in healthy, caring, and purposeful criticism. We consider candor to be the ability to not hold back and always be providing feedback, in a tactful manner. From our observations of many peer performance groups, executive retreats, quarterly and annual planning meetings, and high performing teams, candor is one of the biggest differences in high performing teams and is a big part of what drives success for every team member.

An important factor when discussing candor with a group is the fact that every group member has been selected to be a part of the group. For that reason, everyone has input that has already been identified as a benefit for each of the other group members.

Be it your experience, your background, education, network, or any other reason, your feedback is needed for the betterment of each group member. For that reason, candor is expected out of each member. Not to sound to brash when speaking to a group, but if you are holding back from delivering feedback to one of your group members, you are practicing a lack of integrity. We believe all feedback is a gift, and thus being part of the group deems your feedback valuable and important, and it should be said.

The ability to receive feedback is just as important as the ability to give feedback. Candor requires all members of the group to understand all feedback is a gift. Receiving negative or challenging feedback can be tough. Maturity and personal and professional growth among group members require the ability to receive all feedback in a manner that shows appreciation and understanding among the group members who give the feedback.

The skill of giving and receiving feedback and practicing candor in group meetings is one that requires time to develop. The quicker a group can create trusting environments, where all members feel comfortable sharing open and honest feedback through being candid and vulnerable, the quicker a group will be propelled to achieve success. It is essential for group members and facilitators to discuss candor, describe what it is, and to work on improving candor within the group before, during, and after each meeting.

MINDSET #4: ACCOUNTABILITY

With the above mindsets in mind, there is an absolute guarantee that accountability will be present within your peer performance group. Accountability is the capacity to hold group members responsible for what they say they are going to do and within what time frame they are going to do it. As part of the check-out process in group meetings, we ask members to define what exactly it is they are going to do after the meeting to make an impact on their future. As Ferrazzi explains in his book, the right accountability partner or group is essential to hitting your goals. Sometimes your friends and family are too close to you to hold you truly accountable, but a strong peer performance group can be a powerful reinforcing mechanism.

We recommend you review the above mindsets at each meeting and during each pre-call with the entire group.

APPENDIX:
Finding retreat homes, cabins, lodges, experiences, and activities

The following websites are great for finding homes for large retreats. It is important that you take note of the number of bedrooms and number of beds. Specifically note the number of bedrooms, as guests may not want to share bedrooms. These sites have mobile apps for booking.

- Airbnb Mobile App – www.airbnb.com

- VRBO Mobile App – www.vrbo.com

- HomeAway Mobile App – www.homeaway.com

- Klook Mobile App – www.klook.com

- American Express Fine Hotels & Resorts (because, um, it's American Express) – https://www.americanexpressfhr.com/

As of 2017, here are the top 10 activities that are all group friendly: (Check your city for each of these and their availability. Make sure to call in advance to schedule your group outing.)

1. Top Golf (check your city for availability)

2. Indoor sky diving or real sky diving, bungee jumping, or adventure swings/zip line

3. Indoor cart racing Indy style

4. Hiking (seasonal)

5. Group fitness or yoga

6. Fishing charter

7. Historical museum with guided tour

8. City guided tour or evening ghost/haunted tour

9. Professional sporting events (NBA, NHL, NFL, MLB)

10. Private cooking lessons or brewery, wine, or whiskey tasting.

For more ideas, and an overall great book to read, check out the book Bluefishing by Steve Sims.

APPENDIX:
A conversation about space, creativity, and time

For your haters. Yes, you will have haters, non-believers, or just plain negativity. Here is a message to send to them, or to help you mentally overcome the haters.

It isn't easy to schedule a five- to six-hour meeting with your entire organization, nor is it easy to get individuals to agree to meet for two to three days. The first step is getting people to step outside of their comfort zone and unplug for hours or days. Eliminate all distractions and create an entertaining space for creativity and collaboration to incubate and flourish.

If we study artists, musicians, poets, authors, ultra-successful business people, world leaders, and world class athletes, we learn that one of the biggest differences is the ability to create space for creativity and growth to happen along with a stellar support team behind them.

Those mentioned above all take time to create space for creativity to flourish, ideas to build, and room in their minds to reach an optimal state. For this to happen, space must be given time to build. You must unplug, you must stretch your creativity, and you must surround yourself with a support group of individuals who will help you overcome self-doubt and push you by holding you accountable for your goals.

Space needs time to flourish in our minds. We need to cultivate an environment where our minds can go and relax. This takes time. It takes time to unplug from the day-to-day action of our businesses, families, and friends, and it takes time for space in our minds to clear out for creativity. Once we have that creative space available, ideas will flourish, alternative thoughts will appear, and real change will occur. But you must trust the systems, and commit to allowing time for space to happen. It isn't easy, it isn't automatic, and it certainly isn't guaranteed. Often, you'll have to wait, and you'll have to practice. For those of you who have ever attempted meditation, you know it isn't easy, which is why they recommend beginner meditators start with three to five minutes of sitting and then extending your goals from there as you get more practice. Trust the system and get started!

HEADSPACE: THE BEST MOBILE APP FOR MEDITATION TRAINING, PERIOD.

As we stated earlier, we recommend you download the Headspace app for mediation training. There is an excellent 10-day free course which explains how meditation works, myths about meditation, and videos to show you exactly what you should be feeling and thinking, and that it is okay to thought wonder. Download it to practice creating space. If meditation isn't for you, we get it, but it doesn't hurt to try.

APPENDIX:
It is essential to teach peer performance group members to set S.M.A.R.T. goals, and how to make them S.M.A.R.T.

If you made it all the way through the book and have reached the back of this book, you may feel goal setting to be a basic skill that all members of your groups or innovation storm should possess. However, years of experience has shown us that this will not be the case, and a good meeting facilitator will ensure all goals are S.M.A.R.T. before a meeting has been adjourned.

S.M.A.R.T. goals are defined as simple, measurable, attainable, realistic, and timely. What does this mean?

- All smart goals must be simply defined in one sentence or phrase. A descriptive paragraph or multiple bullets outlining the goal may be added under the first summary sentence of the goal itself.

- Must have one measurable metric that will define success. How will you measure that this goal has been achieved? What's the metric to define the goal as completed?

- Must be attainable and realistic, considering resources, time, money, and technology.

- All goals must have a deadline. They must be defined by when they will be achieved.

As a facilitator, have your members read back their goals aloud to the entire group. You will begin to hear S.M.A.R.T. goals, and if they are not, you will hear gaps. A strong facilitator will ask questions that will provoke the goals to get "smarter."

FACILITATOR QUESTIONS FOR GOAL SETTING SESSIONS:

- How can we break that down to make it more bite sized? (Make it simple.)

- What metric will you track regularly and how will you define when the goal is completed with this metric? (Make it measurable.)

- Do you have the resources to achieve this goal? If so, what are they?

- When will you have this goal achieved by?

APPENDIX:
The host's presentation guidelines & question/answer suggestions to provoke thought

The success of a peer performance group revolves around the host's presentation. The presentation makes or breaks the event. It is imperative that the host prepare thoroughly. Each member of the group invests valuable time away from his/her business to participate in the event, and spends a considerable amount of money to attend and participate, so it's important to make sure that every session is meaningful and valuable. The purpose of this outline is to help the host prepare a presentation for the peer performance group meeting. While the host can anticipate getting help from the facilitator to prepare the presentation, the presentation remains the host's responsibility.

A host's presentation needs to be in writing and available as a handout as well as in presentation format.

Always keep in mind that the host's presentation will be delivered to and discussed with the visiting participants in the peer performance group, and this group serves as the host's advisory board. The role of the visiting group members is to help the host improve his/her business by making recommendations, suggestions, and sharing experiences based on each participant's success or familiarity with a problem, challenge, or issue. It is in the presenter's best interests to identify as many problems, challenges, or issues as possible and present these to the peer performance group for possible resolution and improvement. Of course, it is also important for the host to share his/her business philosophies, strategies, and experiences, both successful and unsuccessful. A big portion of the value of a peer performance group is learning from each participants past experiences.

The host can begin the process of creating a successful presentation by involving other employees and asking some key questions that will help the host identify specific discussion points to bring up during the meeting.

HERE ARE SOME KEY QUESTIONS TO CONSIDER:

- In what way is my business/career/organization falling short of my personal and professional expectations?

- If I could make one or two changes to improve the performance of my business or organization, in what areas would these changes need to occur: personnel, management, communications, marketing, etc.?

- Referencing the above question, what specific changes would I make to improve the performance of my organization or business?

- Which personal/professional goals have I not been able to fulfill with the organization, my career, or my professional life to date?

- As a business owner, executive, or organizational leader, what do I do particularly well? In what ways is the organization most successful? What are our strengths?

- As a business owner, executive, or organizational leader, what don't I do particularly well? In what ways is the organization not successful, or as successful as desired? What are our weaknesses?

- As a business, organization, or entity, what opportunities exist for making improvements, or enhancing my success? Identify the opportunities and explain how they can be brought to fruition, and how they would improve the organization.

- As a business, organization, or entity, what threats do I face in the development of a successful business? Identify the threats, i.e., competition, marketing, personnel, finance, skills, etc. Discuss the plan to minimize these threats.

- Given the opportunity to learn from an experienced group of peers that serves as my advisory board, what topics do I/ we want to discuss? Where do I need help? What do I need to improve?

- How can I get the most benefit from this peer performance group?

- What questions will I need to get answered to say that this interaction with the peer performance group was valuable?

While considering each of the above questions, and answering all that are pertinent, make a list of problems, challenges, issues, and questions that you want to discuss during your presentation to the peer performance group. Organize the topics according to when each should be discussed.

The following outline provides possible discussion points and topics. The host does not need to address each point of the outline. The purpose of the outline is to help the host formulate a successful presentation. Use the outline to generate ideas and discussion points to present to the peer performance group.

YOUR PERSONAL HISTORY & BACKGROUND

Discuss your personal background, as well as that of any partners that are involved in your business. Share whatever information you think the group would like to know. Share information that will help the group understand more about you, your business, and the performance of your business. Topics that you could discuss include:

- Where you grew up

- Where you went to school

- Did you always want to be a business owner?

- What were your career goals, if any?

- How long have you lived in your present city/state?

- Talk about your family. How long have you been married? Age of children?

- Are family members involved in the business, why or why not?

- Are you in business with partners?

- When did it occur to you that you wanted to own your own business, and why?

- Prior to your current role, what kind of work did you do, and how did you feel about that work?

- Did you own a business or businesses prior to this organization?

- Prior to this role, what business experience did you have, if any?

- Presently, what are your career goals?

- Presently, what are your personal and family goals?

- Describe your current lifestyle. How do you spend your

time? Describe what you expect your lifestyle to be in 5 years. How will you spend your time?

- What issues or challenges do you face today that you would like to discuss?

- Describe your hobbies and interests.

- What are your passions? What drives you?

- What is your top three bucket list items? (Yes, we want to know!) Pictures are even better.

- What do you do to take clarity breaks? How long do you break for? Where do you go?

- What do you do for personal development? What is your favorite book this year? All-time? Any other things you do for personal development? Podcasts, articles, events? Please share.

- *Pictures are great for this part of the presentation. Show us who you are!*

YOUR ORGANIZATIONAL HISTORY

Discuss your relationship with your current organization, business, or franchise system. How did you become a part of this organization, and why? Be as specific as possible about your interests in the business and share information that will help the group understand more about why you became a part of this organization. Topics that you could discuss include:

- How and when did you learn about your role?

- Why were you attracted to it?

- Was it easy for you to commit to this role? Did you have to be "sold"?

- Did you invest any money to be in this role or in this organization? How did you fund the investment?

- What did you expect to get out of the relationship?

- Share your start up experience in your new role. What was it like getting started in your new role? What was the business like in the first three months, the first year, and the first three years?

- If you are in your business or role as part of a partnership, talk about the structure and relationship of the partnership. How does it work?

- Knowing what you know today, would you have joined the organization you are in again? Why or why not?

- What issues or challenges relative to your history with your current organization would you like to discuss?

YOUR COMPANY STRUCTURE

Discuss the legal and operational structures of your company. Topics to discuss include:

- Are you incorporated? LLC?

- Who owns the company? If there's more than one owner, what percentage is owned by each?

- When you need legal services or consultation, how are they provided for your company?

- Describe the accounting system for your company. How do you collect money, pay bills, pay payroll, handle invoicing, etc.? Do you have an accounting department? What software programs do you use for accounting purposes?

- Does your company embrace a specific vision and mission? If so, please discuss. If not, perhaps you would explain why.

ORGANIZATIONAL CHART & PERSONNEL PERFORMANCE

In this portion of the presentation, we will ask you, the host, to deep dive with us into your organization by sharing details about the following:

- Discuss your organizational chart and share copies or handouts with your peer performance group.
- Discuss the Management Team. How did you recruit each member of the Management Team?
- How many people work in the business?
  - o Who are they?
  - o Their background.
  - o How did you recruit them?
  - o What do they do – discuss their job responsibilities.
- Assess your Management Team and other company employees.
  - o How well do they do their jobs?
  - o How do you evaluate your personnel?
- How do employees know they are performing to your expectations?
  - o Are they reviewed annually, and if so, how so?

PERSONNEL COMPENSATION & BENEFITS

Discuss your company's compensation plan.

- How do you pay yourself?
- How do you pay your employees?
- What benefits does the company provide to employees?
  - o Does the company provide a retirement plan?
- If you employ people who earn commissions, explain their responsibilities and explain your commission schedule.
- How much training do you provide to your employees? What kind of training do you provide? How do employees get the training they need to be successful in your business?

- How much vacation and personal time off do you provide to your employees? Do they get sick time?

- Does your company publish a personnel handbook? Why or why not? What is its purpose or value in your company?

- Why should an employee work for your business as compared to a competitive business, or any other business?

- Describe any issues and challenges related to your company structure.

YOUR BUSINESS OR ORGANIZATIONAL PERFORMANCE

Discuss your company's performance. Topics to discuss include:

- Discuss your results to date as an organization. How much revenue have you done? Profit?

- Discuss your results for the last calendar year. Were the results higher or lower than your expectations? Why or why not?

- Based on results of the last calendar year, what adjustments have you made for the current calendar year to improve your results?

- List the important milestones in your business.

- What are the most important metrics you look at in your business daily, weekly, monthly, and annually?

  o Provide the most up-to-date metrics for those business.

- How have these metrics changes in the past year and past three years improved or declined? Why? *Please provide data and details into each data point.*

- What steps have you taken to improve your performance? For example, additional training, hiring employees to make up for your own weaknesses, etc.

- What are the numbers that are important to you to measure your results? Which numbers do you track? How do you track them? And when do you know that it's time to do something different to improve the numbers?

- Discuss your financial return as an owner if applicable.

- When did your organization break even?

- When did you reach profitability and what level of profitability?

- How do you evaluate your financial return to date?

- Would you do it again?

- What can you do to improve your financial return?

- Discuss your performance for the current calendar year. Share numbers.

- Share a recent set of financial statements.

- Discuss how you allocate your financial resources for the operation of your business.

- How do you decide how much to commit to advertising, to payroll, etc.

  o Share your overhead costs.

  o Explain whether you rent or own your office or office building.

  o Share your philosophy about expenses and the types of expenses that are appropriate for a business of this type, from your point of view.

- Is cash flow a struggle in your business?

  o If yes, why? What are you doing about it?

  o If it's not a struggle, did it used to be? And if so, how did you move beyond having cash flow problems?

- Evaluate your organization from a high level and from an achievements perspective, at the stage the business or organization is in now.

- o What milestones has your business or organization accomplished since you've been in your current role or with the company, and how have those milestones impacted your business or organization? *This is another great opportunity to include pictures.*

- Where does your business need to innovate?

  - o What innovative disruptions have come to your market place that you had to adjust for?

  - o What disruptions are coming soon in your marketplace?

  - o What are you doing to innovate your business model to prepare for long term growth?

YOUR APPROACH TO THE MARKETPLACE

Discuss your marketing strategies for your organization. Topics for discussion include:

- Discuss the marketplace in which you operate. Explain the demographics and the challenges you face in "attacking" the marketplace as a business owner.

- What kinds of clients are in your market? How are they positioned?

- What is your ideal customer?

  - o Who consumes your product or services?

  - o How has this evolved over time?

  - o What research have you completed to validate this information?

- Are you in a Bull or Bear Market?

- How has the market changed in recent years, or since you became a part of the organization?

- What are your expectations for the future performance of the market?

- o How will it change and when?
- o What will you do when the market changes?
- o What did you do in the past when the market changed?
- How do you generate leads?
  - o Discuss the forms of advertising you use.
  - o What are your favorite marketing strategies and methods?
  - o What used to work that doesn't work as well anymore, and vice versa?
- How much do you pay to generate a lead? Specify the cost by type of lead.
- How have you "attacked" your marketplace? What marketing efforts made a huge splash in your market?
  - o What future endeavors from a marketing perspective do you wish to participate in?
  - o How successful are these endeavors?
- Do you co-market with any other organizations? If so, what do you do?
- What relationships do you have with outside marketing agencies or vendors? Which have been fruitful?
- Discuss your relationship with outside trade organizations in your industry, either industry facing or consumer facing.
  - o How do you participate in those organizations?
  - o What do you attend?
  - o Do you recommend any organizations for the group to attend?
- Explain any special relationships that you have with organizations, trade groups, clients, lenders, or vendors that may be helpful to this peer performance group.

- What are any issues and challenges related to marketing and communications of your business or organization that you are facing or have faced in the past?

Once you have completed the host presentation in full detail and have answered questions from your group members, it is time to begin the request for information portion of the presentation. You can include your requests for information in your slide deck or as additional handouts. For quick reference, here is the format:

- State the opportunity, challenge, hunch, position or person to be discussed, issue, or anything else.

- State the why you are bringing this to the group.

- State any direct facts about this.

- State any history, events, timelines and/or connections to this with your organization, or any connection you personally you have with the thing you are bringing to the group and why it is important for the group to understand this.

- State any feelings you are having about this and why you are feeling this (fear, excitement, doubt, hesitation, optimism, pessimism, guilt, anger, distrust, happiness etc.).

- State any supporting data you have about this.

- State any additional information the group should know.

- State exactly what questions you are asking to the group, and how the group can help.

- State what outcomes you believe this could deliver or not deliver.

The above presentation is meant to guide you through a thought provoking and intensive deep dive into your business or organization. Yes, it will be hard to go into this much detail. However, if you put the work in, the peer performance group you will present this much detail to will learn from you and be able to provide you with a long list of suggestions and improvements. You will walk away from this presentation feeling stronger, more confident, and with a greater appreciation for your achievements and milestones thus far in the lifecycle of your organization, and in your role within your organization.

At the end of Day One, as the host, you will feel a sense of gratitude; you may feel a sense of overwhelm from the round of feedback and validation, but you will feel empowered to think bigger and set bigger goals. The host presentation is an incredible opportunity to pull back the curtain for a trusted board of personal and professional advisors. By being vulnerable, you will build trust with your peers, and you will receive honest and open feedback that will benefit your business or organization, and help you grow personally. You will grow personally by opening and being willing to accept feedback.

Your peer performance group, through the perspective of each group member, will assist you in fixating on goals that will drive your business and eliminate failure from your thought process. Doubt and fear all creep into business owners and organizational leaders. A peer performance group does one of two things: confirms or eliminates those fears. If the fear or doubt is confirmed, then the performance group advised you exactly as you needed, and you may save yourself from a big mistake. In the opposite case, the peer performance group may eliminate the fear and empower you to go out and crush it.

The host presentation will be one of the most impactful and productive days you will have in the history of your organization or your current role.

APPENDIX:
Peer performance group example recruitment letter/benefits of a peer performance group

To whom it may concern,

I am writing this memo to you with the intention of presenting an opportunity I am extremely excited about, and I think you will be too. I am in the process of creating and facilitating a peer performance group and would love nothing more if you would consider joining our group.

A peer performance group is a group of likeminded individuals and professionals who share similar interests to grow and develop themselves and their organizations. They do this by committing to building long-term relationships with accountability partners around them in the form of face-to-face meetings which entail sharing best practices, data, and feelings and working together to set goals and grow both themselves, their leadership skills, and the organizations they have founded or a part of. Peer performance group members practice confidentiality and agree not to compete against each other. They also hold each other accountable by setting goals and reporting back to each other the status of those goals.

A peer performance group is a long-term commitment in which group members agree to push each other, grow together, provide candid feedback, and develop a long-term board of personal and professional advisors for one another. A peer performance group is a life-changing step towards success, and will multiply your performance as a human, as well as multiply the performance of your organization.

The benefits of a peer performance group are accountability, data comparison, validation that what you are doing is exactly what you should be doing or not, profitability, and cost savings by not making mistakes other group members have made. One of the most important benefits of a peer performance group is the therapeutic value of spending time with other likeminded individuals who share the same interests and are going through the same challenges as you are. Small business entrepreneurship and leadership can be tough and both mentally and physically exhausting. A support group acting as a personal and professional advisor can be exactly what you need to remain growth-focused, prevent complacency, and actually add more fulfillment and enjoyment in the journey you are on every day you go to work.

I invite you to explore this opportunity more in depth with me by giving me a call to discuss. I'd like to review our potential group members, the time and financial commitments, the homework/ prep work before each meeting, and my vision for the group. I look forward to hearing from you, and I hope you are as excited as I am about this incredible opportunity.

Please give me a call to discuss more at your earliest convenience.

Best,

Meeting Facilitator

Sources and Inspirations

All the books below were cross-referenced or incredible inspirations for *Disrupt From Within*:

Grant, A. M., & Sandberg, S. (2017). *Originals: how non-conformists change the world*. London: WH Allen.

Ismail, S., Malone, M. S., & Geest, Y. V. (2014). *Exponential organizations: why new organizations are ten times better, faster, and cheaper than yours (and what to do about it)*. New York, NY: Diversion Books.

Silverstein, D., Samuel, P., & DeCarlo, N. (2013). *The innovators toolkit: 50 techniques for predictable and sustainable organic growth*. Hoboken, NJ: Wiley.

Collins, J. (2001). *Good to great: why some companies make the leap... and others don't*. London: Random House.

Wickman, G. (2011). *Traction: get a grip on your business*. Place of publication not identified: Eos.

Sinek, S. (2013). *Start with why: how great leaders inspire everyone to take action*. London: Portfolio/Penguin.

Herold, C. (2016). *Meetings suck: turning one of the most loathed elements of business into one of the most valuable.* Place of publication not identified: Lioncrest Publishing.

Hill, N. (2017). *The law of success.* NY, NY: TarcherPerigee, an imprint of Penguin Random House LLC.

Hill, N. (2017). *Think and grow rich.* S.l.: Crestline Books.

Ferrazzi, Keith. *Who's Got Your Back: the Breakthrough Program to Build Deep, Trusting Relationships That Create Success and Won't Let You Fail.* Broadway Books, 2009.

Sims, Steve. *Bluefishing the Art of Making Things Happen.* North Star Way, 2017.

Drape, Joe. "An Agent of Change." *New York Times* 17 Aug 2014 *Pro Basketball* Web. 26 Oct 2017

King Arthur and the Knights of the Round Table, www.lordsandladies.org/king-arthur-knights-round-table-1.htm.

"Roosevelt's Brains Trust." *Roosevelt's Brains Trust | Armstrong Economics,* www.armstrongeconomics.com/research/economic-thought/economics/roosevelts-brains-trust/.

Elkins, Kathleen. "Legendary Tycoon Andrew Carnegie Credits This Practice for His Riches - and It Can Be Used by Anyone." *Business Insider,* Business Insider, 26 June 2015, www.businessinsider.com/andrew-carnegie-master-mind-principle-2015-6.

"Junto Club." *Benjamin Franklin History,* Historical Society, www.behttp://www.benjamin-franklin-history.org/junto-club/njamin-franklin-history.org/junto-club/.

"The Vagabonds." *The Henry Ford,* The Henry Ford Museum, www.thehenryford.org/collections-and-research/digital-resources/popular-topics/the-vagabonds/.

> *"Leverage the absurd to discover the powerful."*
> *—Tim Ferris, Author of The Four Hour Workweek and Tools of Titans*

Acknowledgements

I owe so much to so many people around me who keep me motivated and inspired, and most importantly, those same people have invested time and resources into keeping me sharp and keeping me on my toes. Without the development that so many people have provided me in the form of training, education, mentorship, and conferences, I would not be where I am today.

For this book, I first want to thank Nick Friedman, President and Co-Founder of College Hunks Hauling Junk & Moving. Nick asked me to learn how to do this and to put my spin on it, and it turned out to be so impactful and so much fun, I knew I wanted to teach others how to do so. Also, I'd like to thank Omar Soliman, CEO, College Hunks Hauling Junk & Moving, for being such a believer in the innovation storm and in peer performance groups that he started telling other people about it. From that point forward, I knew it was going to be impactful because Omar's judgements or intuitions are usually on point.

I want to thank Roman Cowan, COO, College Hunks Hauling Junk & Moving, for always believing in me. Roman constantly is reinforcing to do what you love and do what you are good at, and he has helped me realize both of those things. Without Roman reinforcing certain things, I may have missed out on my true purpose.

I owe so much to two mentors, Joe Bourdow and Thelma Ramey. These two have believed in me and given me the courage to go out there and make it happen. Thank you both so much for the support and the amazing stories, which keep me going.

I owe thanks to famous authors and speakers whose words I listen to or read on a regular basis. Some have podcasts, books, blogs, and articles which play a huge role in my day-to-day motivation and understanding around ebbs and flows of energy, health, and doing deep work. You have taught me gratitude, the benefits of doing deep work, focus, and mental health. Those authors are Tim Ferriss, Tony Robbins, Simon Sinek, Gary Vaynerchuck, Seth Godin, Jim Collins, Adam Grant, Cameron Herold, and so many more.

Lastly, but certainly not least, I want to thank my family for the continuous support of this journey I take them on. I wouldn't be able to do any of this without a supportive family who believes in my crazy dreams and supports me to chase after them. I love you!

About the Author

Justin Waltz is currently the Senior Manager of Franchise Operations at College Hunks Hauling Junk & Moving. He supports a franchise operations team which oversees over 100 locations in the United States and Canada. Justin's primary roles include vendor management, franchise training and onboarding, field coaching, and mastermind and advisory council facilitation. Justin is also the master of ceremonies and executive producer of the College Hunks annual conference and the annual leadership conference. Justin is a two-time franchisee and business owner. Justin's career in franchising started with 1-800-GOT-JUNK? as a truck driver, so Justin holds a unique position of working on the front lines of a franchise location, becoming a franchisee, and being part of a franchisor's corporate headquarters. With this unique perspective, Justin brings a wealth of knowledge and experience to the franchising industry.

Originally from Baltimore, Maryland, Justin now resides in St. Petersburg, Florida. He is a member of the Tampa Bay Wave Entrepreneurship Incubator, as well as on the Board of Advisors of the Towson University College of Business and Economics and an active member of the International Franchise Association.

Justin's meetings are unlike any other you've attended. Filled with fun and energy, you will have a productive day and will walk away feeling rejuvenated and energetic, asking yourself where the time went.

Justin is available for executive facilitation of annual retreats, quarterly planning meetings, and innovation storms. Justin also trains facilitators in innovation storm execution, annual retreats/ quarterly planning meetings, as well as mastermind group meeting facilitation. To contact Justin, email Jw@JustinWaltz.com.

Innovation Storm
Guest Facilitation

If you or your organization are interested in hearing more about having Justin Waltz as a guest facilitator for your innovation storm, please email JW@JustinWaltz.com.

A GUEST FACILITATED INNOVATION STORM INCLUDES THE FOLLOWING:

- ✓ Webinar with leadership team to discuss and determine problem statement.
- ✓ Webinar with all participants to set the stage, announce problem statement, and open for Q&A.
- ✓ Promotional material and announcements leading up to the storm.
- ✓ Storm kit for up to 50 participants.
- ✓ Mindset and rules posters for the meeting space.
- ✓ Live facilitation by Justin Waltz for one day.
- ✓ Recorded and documented questions from the question storm after the event.
- ✓ Recorded and documented ideas after the event.

- ✓ Impact vs. Effort matrix documentation after the event.
- ✓ Follow-up calls to hold implementation strategy session and accountability.
- ✓ Special music and extra learning opportunities for the team.
- ✓ Facilitator coaching for future innovation storms.

We would love to facilitate your innovation storm! Please contact JW@JustinWaltz.com for more information.

Made in the USA
Columbia, SC
09 October 2018